BIG
WEED

BIG

WEED

AN ENTREPRENEUR'S HIGH-STAKES ADVENTURES IN THE BUDDING LEGAL MARIJUANA BUSINESS

CHRISTIAN HAGESETH

WITH

JOSEPH D'AGNESE

palgrave
macmillan

First published in 2015 by PALGRAVE MACMILLAN® TRADE in the
United States–a division of St. Martin's Press LLC, 175 Fifth Avenue, New
York, NY 10010.

Palgrave® and Macmillan® are registered trademarks in the United States,
the United Kingdom, Europe and other countries.

ISBN: 978-1-137-28000-8

Library of Congress Cataloging-in-Publication Data

Hageseth, Christian, 1968–
   Big weed : an entrepreneur's high-stakes adventures in the budding legal
marijuana business / Christian Hageseth with Joseph D'Agnese.
      pages   cm
   Includes index.
   ISBN 978-1-137-28000-8 (alk. paper)
    1. Hageseth, Christian, 1968– 2. Marijuana—United States. 3. Marijuana
industry—United States. 4. Marijuana—Law and legislation—United States.
I. D'Agnese, Joseph. II. Title.
HD9019.M382U645   2015
381'.41379092—dc23
[B]

                                                                    2014040132

Design by Letra Libre, Inc.

First edition: April 2015

10 9 8 7 6 5 4 3 2 1

Printed in the United States of America.

CONTENTS

INTRODUCTION

WHEN I LEFT MY HOUSE ON A BEAUTIFUL MORNING IN February 2013, I was carrying $40,000 in cash in my backpack. The sun was just hitting the foothills of the Rockies as I drove out of Lowry, the neighborhood where I live in Denver. As you might surmise from the contents of the backpack, it was going to be a big day.

My first appointment was the most important. I was meeting with an architect I'd hired several months ago to design a building I was planning to construct somewhere within Denver city limits. The first building of its kind anywhere in the world.

The architect ushered me into his office and we chatted while we looked over the plans together. The model was awesome. I'd never seen anything so beautiful, except perhaps the faces of my children. And this building, in a way, was a child of mine. Any entrepreneur would recognize the feeling I was having. When you have an idea for a business, bringing it into the world takes hard work, money, and imagination. You have to nurture it, just as you would a child.

I was a long way from actually building the place. But all I needed at the moment were detailed drawings and a scale model to sell the dream. People are funny; they have trouble accessing their imaginations. If you don't show them a picture of what you're envisioning, they just won't get it. These images and models were meant to help others see what I saw. With this project, I was going to have to sell the dream to a lot of people: current shareholders, future investors, regulators, my employees, and the media. I would turn to this model again and again to show my vision to many people along the way.

And here in front of me, my vision had come to life: a visitors' center with 50-foot-high cathedral ceilings; a restaurant and bar overlooking the outdoor amphitheater and greenhouse; a gift shop; an engaging behind-the-scenes tour open to the public; and cottages for visiting musicians, artists, and craftspeople. The whole facility would be powered by the cleanest, greenest energy we could find. I intended to shoot for LEED Platinum status, the highest green building certification in the construction business.

I had poured all my hope and energy into this place. Someday, when my customers walked in and were surrounded by glass and stone and light, when they were confronted with a 40-foot-high wall of living plants and heard the trickling of the indoor waterfall that flowed over the face of the Green Man—the emblem of my company—I wanted them to be struck by one awesome fact:

This place is special. It's a cathedral to the Mother Nature aspect of God. We are all connected to Nature. We share it together and cannot be separated from it.

"By the way," I told the architect, "I brought your money."

I started placing 1-inch stacks of hundred-dollar bills on his desk. "Whoa!" he said. "What are you doing?"

"What does it look like? I'm paying you."

"Dude, we talked about this. It has to be by check. Otherwise we're going to have a problem." He leaned forward, his face suddenly anxious and awkward. That face? I know that face very well. I've seen it countless times since getting into this industry five years ago. "Chris, you know I can't take this. It's *drug* money."

Oh. Yeah. I forget sometimes.

I should back up and explain something. My name is Christian Hageseth and I sell marijuana for a living. Honest-to-goodness, *legal* marijuana. That building my architect just designed for me? It's destined to be the world's first weedery. Not a winery. Not a brewery. A weedery. A $30 million tourist destination. A chance to get inside the action with America's newest and fastest-growing industry.

When I started my business, Green Man Cannabis, in 2009, I sold medical marijuana. My customers were people who suffered from nausea following rounds of chemotherapy. Or they had crippling migraines. Some had old surfing injuries that still flared up and threatened to ruin their days. All these people and more stopped by one of our dispensaries and allowed us to sell them some bud. With our product in hand, they were able to light up, toke away, and start feeling better in minutes.

We grossed about $300,000 that first year. In 2014, when recreational marijuana became legal in the state of Colorado and any resident over the age of twenty-one could walk in and buy up to an ounce of weed without fear of being busted by the cops, sales throughout the state jumped. We grossed $4 million that year, and our firm wasn't even catering to the recreational market. Not yet, anyway. I was holding back, biding my time until we were ready and I could roll out something so unforgettable that every marijuana smoker or enthusiast in the world would want to see for themselves.

When the weedery, which we will hereafter call the Green Man Cannabis Ranch, comes online, we anticipate doing about $97 million in revenue in our first year. That's the radical leap in revenue that all businesses hope for but few ever realize. We will be able to do it because we were in the right place at the right time, operating a business that was doing things the right way. Everything in our company's past had led inevitably to this big moment.

We weren't alone. Since marijuana first became legal in 2000, the state of Colorado has issued nearly a thousand marijuana licenses. People are fond of saying that there are more places to buy legal marijuana in Colorado than there are Starbucks. But despite its seeming ubiquity, the cannabis industry has a long way to go. It is still a little rough around the edges. Still has a lot of kinks to iron out. One of those kinks is what to do with all the cash the industry generates. Cash that makes people like my architect nervous.

What he'd just said—*It's drug money!*—hung in the air between us.

"Look," I said. "You don't have a problem. You're being paid for your architectural services. *I'm* the one who's being paid for marijuana. You don't have a problem—*I* do."

"When we first started working together, we agreed. You agreed to pay by check."

Yeah, I did. And I had wanted to honor that request. I really did, just as I have for every vendor of ours who made the same request. But the law of the land at the time didn't allow us to enjoy the benefits of banking. In my business, marijuana and banks don't mix.

In 2009, the state of Colorado racked up such a huge marijuana slush fund that it was able to reach in and help itself to $3 million to balance the state budget. In 2010, it used $9 million from the same fund to do it again. The state was facing a $60 million shortfall because it was not receiving as much federal Medicaid assistance as it had in the past. (This had nothing to do with the world of medical marijuana, by the way; it was just federal budget cutting as usual.) Governor Bill Ritter admitted that he had opposed making medical marijuana legal, but when the chips are down, cash is cash. Thanks to more than 150,000 state residents who had paid fees into the medical marijuana program cash fund to be allowed access to medical weed, and we "ganjapreneurs," as we were sometimes called, who supplied the product, the state's butt was saved. Capitalism had ridden in on a big, green, sticky horse and saved the day. Yay, weed.

But those of us in the industry were still not allowed to carry a checkbook.

Oh, I could convert our hard-earned company cash into a paper check if I tried hard enough, but it was always a hassle.

"I did promise to bring you a check," I said, "but we just can't make it happen right now. Sorry."

"Let me call my lawyer."

The architect dialed and talked while I studied the sunlight streaming through the windows of his tony office. I didn't wait for his lawyer's reply. I already knew what it would be. I just stuffed the cash back into my backpack.

Well, it was certainly worth a try. But now I had a problem. I was downtown for the rest of the day. I had a raft of other pressing appointments. It would be hours before I reached one of the safes I had sprinkled around town to safeguard my company's cash. Shoot. And at lunch I was taking my usual yoga class.

What was I going to do, stuff the cash in my yoga locker? Even yogis aren't that honest.

FOR THIRTEEN YEARS—from 1920 to 1933—alcohol was banned in the United States. The government cracked down on the production and consumption of a host of intoxicating beverages. Law-abiding Americans who used to drink and still managed to hold jobs, pay taxes, love their children, and have decent lives sat back and watched as their nation expended a good deal of fruitless energy cracking down on a product that—in the hands of responsible adults—was less harmful than trying to enforce draconian laws of absolute abstinence. In the absence of legitimate businesses distilling and selling alcohol to the American public, organized crime sprung up to supply demand. Finally, the American government saw the error of its ways. Prohibition was repealed, and the booze started flowing again.

The legalization of marijuana is like the ending of Prohibition.

Right now, as I write this, medical marijuana is legal in twenty-five states and the District of Columbia in the United States of America. More than 50 percent of the American population could, if they qualify and are inclined to do so, get what amounts to a prescription from their doctor, walk into a state-licensed dispensary, buy some marijuana, go home, and get high without fear of arrest and prosecution.

Four of those states—Alaska, Colorado, Oregon, and Washington—currently allow or will soon allow the purchase and consumption of *recreational* marijuana. That means if you're an adult, you can buy and use marijuana the way you buy and use tobacco and alcohol, or the way grown-ups walk into a casino on a weekend getaway and play the slots without worrying about cops raiding the place. Recreational marijuana initiatives are on the ballots or being considered by legislators in at least five more states. The handwriting is on the wall. Recreational marijuana may very well be coming to a state near you.

Maybe you love marijuana. Maybe you're against it. Regardless, you have to admit that we are watching history in the making. We are privileged to watch a profound shift in the American way of life. Remember that old saying: "May you live in interesting times"? Well, we are doing just that, and we should sit up and try to understand what those times are telling us.

This book is about my time on the front lines of the cannabis movement. It's the story of a nascent industry that is experiencing growing pains. It's the story of lawmen, politicians, bureaucrats, and judges who are dealing with a whole new set of rules governing public behavior. It's the story of vacationers, partiers, hobbyists, and fun seekers who have a new toy in their arsenal to use, abuse, experiment with, and decide if it's for them. It's the story of athletes and businessmen who are itching to invest in the Next Big Thing. But mostly, it's the story of a business guy trying to chase a dream and the entrepreneurs and investors like him who are dying to leap into a new world of opportunity.

I call it the world of Big Weed because it's a whole new way of thinking about a product that was once the scourge of the nation. Marijuana is an ancient plant whose cultivation by humans stretches back at least ten thousand years. But for our purposes, the "Old

World" of marijuana only reaches back to the 1930s, when propaganda films such as *Reefer Madness* tried to scare Americans away from a plant whose use, it was said, would drive them insane and turn them into murderers, prostitutes, or worse. The Old World was the age of President Richard Nixon, who ignored the scientific consensus on this relatively benign plant and instituted a wrongful drug policy that would doom millions of Americans to prison for possession—and is still in effect today. With the stroke of a pen, millions more non-Americans were sentenced to die as a result of drug cartel violence that sprang up to circumvent the American war on drugs. The Old World, then, was a mix of good and bad. On one hand, it was hippies and stoners, psychedelic art, Woodstock, marijuana-leaf posters, and getting high in your parents' basement. On the other, it was also the beginning of untold violence and lost opportunities for the American underclass.

The "New World" of weed is a far cry from all that. It's a world in which private equity firms carefully study the historical financials and business plans of marijuana start-ups to see if they would like to invest a few million dollars of their money on this hot new industry. It's a world in which law-abiding citizens check into pricy bed and breakfasts for the weekend in the Rocky Mountains and legally smoke a joint while relaxing naked in a hot tub. It's a more compassionate world, where chronically or terminally ill patients have access to a natural product that can help safely ameliorate some of the symptoms of their diseases. It's a world where the company that wins the public relations challenge, and sells America its favorite marijuana, has a very real shot at being a lifestyle brand, as big and as warmly embraced as Sam Adams, Apple, or Starbucks.

The industry is about two years away from beginning to see record profits. Imagine if you had been about to buy into the world of gourmet coffee (Starbucks), online retail (Amazon), or personal computers (Apple) two years before these businesses revolutionized the world. Would you have done so? Would you have sat up and listened to what Howard Schultz, Jeff Bezos, or Steve Jobs had to say?

The New World of marijuana has some monster players too. After all, if marijuana is legal, Big Tobacco will want a piece of the action. So will Big Pharma and Big Agra, companies that will want to study and quantify and possibly patent various elements of this precious plant's genome. In fact, it's already happening.

As I write this, I'm forty-five years old. For years, I went to work in a suit and tie, but these days it's mostly cargo shorts, a comfortable shirt, flip-flops, and my mala beads. And yeah, I smoked marijuana as a kid, and I smoke it now. I'm sorry if that's a problem for you, but it's integral to what I'm about to tell you.

But that's not the whole of my story. In college I got hooked on a different rush—greed, status, and ego—and I ended up channeling it all into business. I did well in whatever businesses I started, like a lot of people who are driven by the same things. I didn't implode the way some folks do, but I came close.

Eventually, my eyes were opened and I saw my greed for what it was: the empty, vain pursuit of a hollow man. These days, after two decades of running different types of businesses, I like to tell people that marijuana has been my salvation. I mean that. The cannabis business appeared on my horizon when I needed it most, when I was at a difficult crossroads in my career, and the business has given me nothing but joy.

What success I had in my earlier businesses was probably due to the fact that I am restlessly creative. Following other people's direction has never worked well for me. I had to find my own way, my own path in business. They call people like me entrepreneurs. Entrepreneurship is what I know, what I do, what I breathe. In fact, it's all I've ever known since the day I graduated college and opened my first company, a string of ice cream shops. I don't make music, paint, or tell stories—my creativity is expressed through business, through making deals, through working with other people. Entrepreneurship is my creative expression and my passion.

Today, my indoor grow facilities are brimming with tall, beautiful plants. Some of our marijuana strains are seven times more potent than what the hippies smoked in the 1960s. I sell our harvest at our two medical dispensaries in Denver. Green Man Cannabis has twice won the Cannabis Cup, the highest award for excellence in the legal marijuana industry. These days I've gotten comfortable with potential investors asking me if I can send them a business plan. If you think it's strange that a "drug dealer" would be handing out prospectuses, then you've got a lot to learn about the world of legal weed.

As I go about my business every day, a lot of honest, law-abiding people can't help asking me a ton of questions.

"You're in the legal marijuana business?" they say with a grin on their faces. "What's that like?"

This book is my attempt to answer that question.

Because it was one of the first states to legalize marijuana, Colorado makes a nice case study for what will or could be soon happening in a state near you and around the globe in places like Uruguay—which just became the first country in the world to make marijuana completely legal within its borders—and Israel, which is funding serious research into the healing properties of marijuana. I'm going to share how I got into the business and how I turned Green Man Cannabis into the success it is. You'll watch my ups and downs, my outright failures, and you'll get a feel for the pros and cons of the new world.

I hope this book speaks to a lot of different people. But those who'll get the most out of it are people like these:

- entrepreneurs of all stripes who are considering starting any new venture, or who are considering entering the cannabis industry in particular

- investors who have heard from their friends, attorneys, and accountants that cannabis is the hot new thing but who are hesitant about parting with their money until they learn more about the industry
- middle managers and small business owners who are interested in seeing how someone made the transition from a small business to a multimillion-dollar corporation
- employers who are interested in motivating or educating staffers with stories of success
- longtime marijuana lovers (and haters) who are intrigued by the big business that has literally grown around this strange little plant
- observers who are fascinated by the shift in American society and who are eager to learn more

For all its seeming sophistication, the industry is also in a bit of a Wild West phase right now. On one hand, you've got entrepreneurs like me who are racing to establish market share. On the other hand, you've got cops, judges, and state regulators who are trying to figure out what legal marijuana means for their hallowed institutions. How do we decide case law? How do we regulate it? And the fact that it's still a federal crime to grow and sell marijuana has huge implications beyond my inability to carry a corporate checkbook.

Though most of my business dealings are privileged information, I will take you inside some of my meetings and conference calls to show you how it all goes down. You will meet a bizarre cast of characters in this book. For every Wall Street suit who's dreaming of a piece of the big old marijuana brownie, there's a colorful millionaire—a captain of industry or hip-hop star or an athlete—who is ringing my phone off the hook, wanting to invest in this burgeoning trade.

But the way I see it, the real heroes of this story are *money* and the American public.

Why do I say that? Look at it this way: When I was a kid, you could gamble legally in only two places in the United States: Atlantic City and the state of Nevada. Today you can enjoy a casino experience in twenty states in the country, and some form of gambling—racetracks, lotteries, scratch-off cards—are found in forty-eight U.S. states. Why? Money. As much as the powers that be hated vice, they hated losing potential tax revenue more.

Here's where the American public comes in. Consumers changed the history in the past simply by broadening their minds. In the 1930s, Americans toppled Prohibition. And they gradually let their lawmakers know that they were open to the idea of legalized gambling. The legislators listened. They *had* to.

Well, today we're in the same position with marijuana. The citizens of the United States were once content to believe what the federal government told them about the evils of marijuana. Now that they're older, wiser, and have a few tokes under their belts, voters are less likely to be snowed. They know in their guts that the drug policies of the past forty years have failed massively and that it just might be time for their nation to try something new. Every time a voter hears someone—a politician, an activist, or some other naysayer—rail against marijuana, the voter is likely to think "Well, I smoked marijuana a couple of times, and nothing bad happened. I didn't get hooked on cocaine. I hold down a decent job. I make decent money. I have a house, a mortgage, and kids. Ergo, methinks you're full of shit."

Think about that: The thing that was once so evil is now being regarded as something responsible adults can enjoy, just the way they occasionally smoke, drink, or gamble.

For decades, marijuana was in the hands of an underground culture—stereotyped as hippies and stoners—but it's now shifting into the hands of mainstream America.

What's that mean? For one thing, it means that the *story* of marijuana in the twenty-first century will be told by people like me.

Sit down, light up a joint, and let me tell you about my world.

1

BRAVE NEW WORLD

IT ALL STARTED THE WAY A LOT OF BUSINESSES BEGIN—
on the golf course.

The year was 2009, and I was between jobs. My attorney and good friend thought it might be a good idea for me to meet a client of his. He invited us to come play at the Red Rocks Country Club, one of the nicer country clubs in Denver, nestled in the same geologic formation as the iconic Red Rocks Amphitheatre.

The guy I met, Jake, was a stocky Latino, with the build of a boxer.

"What kind of business are you in?" I said.

"You'll like this," my lawyer said, with a smile on his face.

"Marijuana," Jake said. "Legal, medical marijuana."

Oh yeah, I thought. I'd heard something about it, only in the vaguest way. I was a citizen of Colorado. I read the papers. I watched TV. And I knew what the average citizen knew: Voters had approved a law allowing medical marijuana back in 2000. Since then, the cannabis industry had risen from home growers cultivating a few plants on behalf of a few patients to a small number of professional dispensaries scattered throughout the state. But that was about all I knew. I had never set foot in one of those places. I knew nothing about the business. I was a businessman with a wife and three kids. And when medical marijuana was in its infancy, I was busy running a real estate enterprise.

That said, I also was no angel. When I wanted to get high—and I did, from time to time—I bought my weed the old-fashioned way. From a buddy.

"As a matter of fact, gentlemen," I said, rooting around in one of the pockets of my golf bag, "I have some on me right now."

With a flourish, I whipped out a wooden "one-hitter," a small wooden box that had both a small metal pipe and a small storage area that contained some ancient street weed. I had no idea when I'd bought this marijuana or how long it had lain hidden in the confines of my bag. I was just foolishly proud of the fact that I had it. Like I was some cool businessman living on the edge. Counterculture and proud.

Well, Jake took one look at that shit and shook his head. "Check *this* out."

He produced his own Ziploc bag and handed it over.

My God, there was no comparison. My weed was nearly black with age and smelled like the ass of a mummified skunk.

Jake's weed consisted of plump, sticky buds that were bright green and shot through with fine tendrils of floral color. They looked exactly like what they were: the flowers of a beautiful, generous plant.

"Where did you get this?" I said. *I needed to know his guy!*

Jake just laughed.

I looked over my shoulder to be sure we were alone. On a weekday in summer, a golf course can be one of the most deserted places on the planet.

"Can we smoke this here?" Jake asked my attorney.

Well, we did, and we were still smoking when we got to the seventeenth hole, and let me tell you: Oh, wow. The beautiful view from the seventeenth hole at Red Rocks County Club just became that much more spectacular. Looking down the fairway as it disappeared out of sight, the tall buildings of downtown Denver seemed to be just beyond the hole.

Holy shit.

The second I took that first puff, my mind expanded. And I don't mean that in the woo-woo, New Agey sense. I mean it in the practical sense.

One puff, and I knew.

I could smell, feel, and taste the difference between the street weed I'd smoked as a kid and the prime stuff lovingly created by someone who knew what he was doing.

It was like night and day.

Like the difference between that $8.99 cabernet sauvignon you tossed in your shopping cart at the supermarket because you needed some wine, any wine, tonight with dinner and that amazing bottle the sommelier brought to your table last year when you wanted something special for your anniversary.

Like the difference between a hastily gobbled Snickers bar and a nibble of an artisanal bar of hand-crafted chocolate with 70 percent cocoa content.

Like the difference between Coors Light on a hot summer's day and a microbrew crafted with the freshest hops possible and a few other things you didn't even know you could put in beer.

Like that.

Holy shit, I thought. I've been smoking ditch weed all my life.

"You should stop by," Jake said. "We can help you get your red card."

I didn't even know what that meant.

Maybe you're like me. When I get excited, I start thinking about possibilities. Opportunities. Implications. It took me all of ten minutes to go from a guy falling in love with what was getting him high to a business guy with some pretty obvious questions.

"What's it cost to grow?"

Jake squinted as he lined up his shot. "Um, it varies."

"Well, what's your margin?" He looked quizzical. "Your profit," I said, trying to make myself clearer. "The difference between what it costs you to grow and what you sell it for. That tells you how much profit you're gonna make."

"Well . . . I don't know exactly, but the business has been great so far."

I looked at my attorney.

He smiled.

Jake was a nice guy. Medical weed was only his most recent endeavor. He had started a franchise restaurant, made it successful and sold it off, so he knew a good bit about business. And he knew a lot about weed. He had learned how to run somebody else's business, but was he up to the challenge of creating something out of nothing? That is an entirely different skill set. It also happened to be *my* skill set.

Jake, incidentally, has come a long way. As I write this, he and I are the respective chief executive officers of two of Colorado's largest legal marijuana companies. We see each other occasionally at industry events and recently we met with the governor of Colorado together. But that day on the golf course, he needed some help, so I agreed to do a brief consulting gig with his firm.

In that moment, though, before my buzz dissipated, I saw an entirely different business in my mind's eye. I saw it as if it had already been built. They say that Michelangelo saw David inside that marble slab and only had to help the statue find its full expression. That's how I felt when I realized what a great marijuana company could be like.

A FEW DAYS LATER, I was sitting in the office of a physician who worked in Colorado's growing medical marijuana trade.

If you wanted to buy medical marijuana in the state of Colorado, you needed to have a red card—official proof that you had jumped through all the hoops. Doctors didn't write "prescriptions" for the stuff, they wrote "recommendations."

The doctor Jake hooked me up with was in his eighties. Kind eyes. Fuzzy gray hair loping over the tops of his ears. "So what's troubling you?"

Where do I start? The poor doc didn't have enough time in the day to hear it all. Did he really want to hear how I'd lost my company more than a year ago when the market crashed? Did he really want to hear how I'd almost brought home a seven-figure payday—and then didn't?

"Anxiety," I said, hitting upon a diagnosis he could probably use. "I have trouble sleeping. Been through a tough time lately. Does anxiety work?"

"No," he said. "It has to be one of the six qualifying conditions approved by the state, a *physical* ailment that the marijuana can help you treat."

That was marijuana's gift to the world, its raison d'être in the new medical marketplace. While the rest of us prized it for its ability to get us high, there were people living with chronic illness—cancer patients, AIDS patients, to name a few—who wanted marijuana for its ability to extinguish pain, stimulate appetite, and banish nausea.

Wait. Back in my youth I'd suffered an injury in a snowboarding accident and compressed a thoracic vertebrae in my back. The injury still bugged me. So much so that I used an inversion table to hang myself upside down from time to time. Stretching myself out was one of the only ways I'd found to chase the pain and numbness away.

"That'll do," the doctor said.

He initiated the paperwork and helped me fill out the state application. I stepped outside to get it notarized by someone in his office. Next, I needed to stop by the post office and mail it in to the state via registered mail. But I could walk out of the doctor's office right now and buy up to 2 ounces of weed per visit.

It sounded too good to be true. In fact, a lot of habitual marijuana users thought so, too. That's why they stuck with buying their weed off the street.

As I was about to leave, I lingered in the doctor's office. I have a soft spot in my heart for docs. My dad was a former U.S. Navy flight surgeon. In December 1968, he soloed for the first time, earning his wings. The very next day, he delivered me at the hospital at the Naval Air Station in Pensacola, Florida. I grew up all over the United States—North Carolina, Washington, California, and finally Colorado. Ours was an interesting childhood, to say the least, but a distinctly middle-class one. The thought of an elderly doctor willing to write recommendations for marijuana struck me as odd.

"If you don't mind my asking," I said, "why do you do this?"

He shrugged and gave me another smile. "I always thought marijuana was harmless. I'm glad I'm able to finally do this for people."

NOW THAT I HAD A RED CARD in my pocket, I could legally enter any marijuana dispensary in the state. My first visit to Jake's business impressed the hell out of me. Imagine walking in and hitting a wall of that powerful marijuana scent. Once again, I was blown away by the contrast between the smell of street weed and fresh marijuana.

Jake's crew had about ten tall glass jars, maybe a half gallon each, with latch lids on them, crammed with fat, healthy, colorful buds.

His staff—people who called themselves "budtenders"—blew my mind when they asked me a single question: "What kind of marijuana do you like to smoke?"

Well, shit, I didn't even have the mental framework to be able to answer that question. As far back as I could remember, there was only one kind of marijuana and you got it from a buddy . . . who knew a guy who knew a guy who was going to pick some up from his friend today. So, if you brought your money by now, your buddy would have it later today. And sometimes those best-laid plans just didn't go down.

I remember being just a kid, about twelve years old, the first time I saw my older brother and his friends giggling over a black plastic film canister he was holding in his hands.

"What's that?" I asked them.

"Nothing! Mind your own business." They blew me off, dashed into my brother's bedroom, and locked the door behind them.

But I didn't give up. "What's that?" I asked the next time I saw them toting one of those little canisters.

Nothing. Silence.

And then one day, my brother blurted, "It's just grass." The smirk on his face gave it away.

It's just grass.

It's just grass.

And then one day, they let me have a little toke. Wow. I laughed for the next few hours.

I smoked in junior high and even high school. Not often, and I never allowed it to interfere with my relatively normal life. I played football and rugby and hung out with the jocks and preppies more than the stoners.

But the memory of marijuana still remained with me, as did the whole marijuana experience. The semi-ridiculous dance of calling around all of your friends to see if anyone knew someone who had some. Finally finding that one buddy . . . who knew the guy who knew a guy. Then hammering out a price. Pulling together all the crumpled fives, tens, and singles you and your friends could muster. The meet. The buy. The furtive smokefest in your parents' basement, always accompanied by the post-toke, rapacious romp through the pantry. Lots of laughter. Music. TV. The paranoia that sometimes gripped us: Would someone notice our red eyes, our incessant laughter, or the remnants of our outing?

That was the 1980s for me.

The marijuana we smoked as kids was always sourced the same way. We had one choice, paid one price when we were lucky enough to get to the guy who knew the guy.

But here in Jake's dispensary, I was beginning to learn that there were lots of different types of marijuana. Different strains. Each with different names and different personalities.

I had a lot to learn, but right now I needed to get down to business. I needed about five or six hours with Jake to figure out how his business actually worked so I could put together a spreadsheet that spelled it all out.

The numbers were fascinating. It cost vendors like Jake about $500 to $800 to grow a pound of legal marijuana. That probably sounds like a lot of money. It did to me. But what did I know? A plant is a plant is a plant. People grew tomatoes and lettuce in their backyards each summer, and it wasn't rocket science. I didn't understand why marijuana had to be that much more difficult or expensive. The kicker was guys like Jake could turn around and sell one of those same pounds—at a quarter-ounce at a time—for $6,400 retail. Or he could sell a pound for about $4,000 wholesale at that time.

A profit margin of 800 percent to 1,300 percent. Un-fucking-believable!

The numbers looked good for a retail business. Really good.

So much so that I couldn't get the marijuana business out of my head even after my consulting gig with Jake was up. I was talking about it with everyone I met.

What surprised me was that, although everyone in the upper-middle-class suburban social circle I hung out in had heard that medical marijuana was now legal, very few people had had much experience with it. They'd say the most ridiculous things when I brought it up.

"I know it's legal, but you can't really buy it, can you?"

"It's still against the law, though, isn't it?"

"I don't care if it's legal—it's still wrong!"

And on and on.

I remember the first time my then wife confronted me about it. "What's with this marijuana stuff?" she said.

"It's going to be huge," I said. "It's an amazing opportunity. I am going to take some time and look into it."

"You have children," she reminded me. "You have a family. You need to get a job and bring home a paycheck!"

She had grown up in a fairly conservative Colorado family. Sure, like a lot of people her age, she had smoked marijuana, but she didn't like it, and that was that. Marijuana was wrong. It was something stoners, losers, and criminals did. She didn't see why I found it intriguing. And she had a very different risk tolerance. My entrepreneurship had always made her uncomfortable. Being an entrepreneur in the weed business *really* made her uncomfortable.

You don't have time to be wasting on bullshit "opportunities," she thought.

We have five mouths to feed.

We have an expensive lifestyle with a mortgage and a couple of cars to pay for.

Chris, what you need right now is a good job.

A real job.

With a decent paycheck.

You know—like the one you used to have.

APPARENTLY I USED TO BE SOMEBODY. A contender. A mover. A shaker.

Once I was the founder and CEO of a national real estate company. During the booming housing market, which lasted from 2002 to 2008, I developed a novel way of financing pools of real estate. I had executed it only a couple of times before forming a company to do more, similar deals. You can only structure so many securities before you exhaust your exemptions with the Securities and Exchange Commission. If I wanted to keep using this method, I had to launch a public offering. I'd never done such a thing. I was thirty-eight years old at the time and a self-made millionaire.

I'd spent the last six years building a real estate corporation initially devoted to increasing the value of residential real estate. As the housing market started heating up in the United States, my company began buying properties all over the country. The demand for housing was insatiable, and it seemed as if every investor and bank on the planet was throwing money at us.

Our process was fairly simple. Basically, we'd assemble a group of, say, twenty investors, each of whom would buy one property. Each investor would then contribute the property in a tax-deferred exchange into a limited partnership. Then the pool of properties would be managed and eventually sold or exploited for their cash-flow potential. The owners of the limited partnership would then receive the benefit of the sale or the cash flow that stemmed from the rent we were charging our tenants. A structure like this allowed each investor to spread the risk over the entire pool of properties. This diversification of risk and normalization of return was the premise I'd built my business upon. And it had worked wonderfully—until it didn't.

Everything I'd done in the last six years was building up to that public offering, with a net asset value of $1 billion.

My company stood to earn $17 million at offering alone and much more over time.

And I, the humble servant to this paragon of American entrepreneurship, would be taking home a solid seven-figure payday to my loving wife and three adorable daughters.

I made this happen.

I had it coming to me.

I had earned it.

It was American capitalism at its best.

Yeah, I know now: I and my investor buddies had just partici-pated in the biggest real estate fuck-up in the history of American business. We just didn't see it.

The first glimmers of the collapse, in fact, were barely noticeable.

Some people saw it on Wall Street. Me, I learned about it first-hand from the comments the SEC tacked onto the first set of docu-ments we sent describing our public offering. It asked us to get the financing underwritten.

"No problem," I said.

I'd done this hundreds of times and had connections throughout the industry. I started taking meetings with the lenders with whom I had worked over the last several years, thinking it would be an easy sell. But every time I wrapped my pitch, they'd be sitting there, star-ing at me, with an awkward grin on their faces.

Yeeaahhhh, that look said, we're not going to be investing in that anymore. The market's turning . . .

I figured they were just skittish, so I took more meetings. Guys, do you see the opportunity here? A billion fucking dollars. Can you smell that, guys? We are within a month of the offering! We've been working on this for more than a year . . .

Crickets.

It took me only a few meetings to realize that nobody was biting. That no one would ever bite again. The worm had turned. The indus-try was sunk. My company was in over its head and heading toward bankruptcy. We had spent a majority of our cash reserves on the costs of the public offering. My personal assets were safe; I'd wisely kept them apart from those of the company. But now I had to dismantle the behemoth I'd created. It took me fifteen months to shut the whole thing down, while, on the sidelines, millions of other less fortunate investors were scrambling to save themselves and their skins.

Fifteen months of shucking off what I had worked so hard to create and what everyone in America was now regarding as the world's worst idea ever.

I tried to be philosophical about the loss. After all, business was in my blood. I'd started that chain of ice cream shops when I was fresh out of college. Then I'd sold them and moved on to another business, then another and another. It was what I did. I was an entrepreneur. Guys like me don't just go out and get a job. We look for opportunities and we create businesses where there are none. People, products, and services are our paint, brush, and canvas. Creating those companies is what inspires us.

But something had changed inside me. Something I had rarely spoken about, even to my wife.

When I was dismantling my latest company, I came across some documents that forced me to rethink the course of my entire life. Among them was a list of my company's assets on one particular day: September 30, 2006. Looking it over, it occurred to me that if I had stopped buying properties on that day alone and sold off everything, my company would have escaped the housing crash unscathed.

Why didn't you stop, Chris? I asked myself.

The answer, when it came, was hard to stomach.

Because it wasn't enough.

What *was* enough, Chris?

I didn't know. The sick fact was that, at the time I was gobbling up those properties, I was a thirty-eight-year-old who had never learned the meaning of *enough*. If I made $1 million, I'd want $10 million. If I made $10 million, I'd want $100 million. If I made $100 million, I'd want $1 billion. And I was closing in on that billion, for my company at least, when it all tanked.

My goals in life had consisted of running toward a finish line painted with a dollar sign.

Some nights I couldn't sleep, thinking of how I was going to move the next mountain to expand our holdings. The daily stress had been so unbearable that I'd nearly ruined my health. I was lucky to have escaped alive.

And now, as I looked out over the ashes of that company, I had to wonder: What was the point of it all?

I realized I had measured my success in dollars, not the joy of living. I had chased wealth and status, not happiness and love. I hardly recognized the man I'd been.

And with that realization, a simple yet profound shift occurred inside me.

I saw with utter clarity that money was meaningless. I already knew how to make it anytime I wanted. In my career, I had earned it, lost it, and earned it back again. If money was that easy to make and lose, money could not be the focus of my life. There were things far more rare and more precious than money. *Those* were the things I ought to cherish, because they would only come around once in a blue moon.

Above all things, I wanted to be a loving and grateful husband and father.

If I was going to start a new business, I wanted to be in harmony with myself. I had to feel integrity.

I wanted to work with passion and purpose.

I wanted to create something that I loved and wanted to share with the world.

I wanted to be a good steward of my community.

I wanted to foster good careers—with good longevity—for my employees.

Money was nice, but if I had money without joy in all these areas of my life, then the money was worth much less. I might as well toss it out and start all over again—just as I had already done many times before.

BUT AS I SAY, my epiphany was not something I talked about openly with my wife, my friends, or my extended family. The bankruptcy had shaken up my wife. She was scared about our future. My getting a decent job and a decent paycheck was the only way she could see us moving forward. Such things represented stability to her.

I didn't want to give her more cause for alarm.

But legal weed was looking more and more like a smart thing to do.

I shared my thinking with people I trusted. One of them was a neighbor of mine I'll call Mr. Pink. He was an accountant, but not just an accountant. A *forensic* accountant. The sort of person the FBI or district attorneys called in to investigate the books of people they'd arrested for financial crimes. The fact that he could apply his intellect to someone else's illegal misdeeds and tell you exactly how it had been pulled off made him something of a badass in my eyes. On top of it, Mr. Pink is a great guy. Barrel chested and larger than life, he is memorable in a good way. Gregarious, engaging, and kind to children. We got along well; Mr. Pink knew money and opportunities when he saw them, and he liked what he was hearing about the legal marijuana trade.

"How much?" he'd say when I told him what people were earning.

His wife would snap, "Don't even think about it."

His wife was a lawyer, and she took the same view my wife did: It was insane to contemplate a career selling legal weed. Colorado's law had been enacted on a whim, and it was liable to be repealed. And when it did, what would happen to all those people who had jumped into it feet first? They'd be rounded up and sent to jail. Or they'd lose their shirts.

Drugs were drugs. People killed people over this stuff.

Marijuana, in other words, was not a suitable business for a white, upper-middle-class guy from Denver.

And as much as Mr. Pink and I would hear those words or glean the subtext from what our wives were saying, we couldn't help dreaming about what a gold mine this was.

"Oh my God," Mr. Pink would say on those occasions when we spoke about it. "We should totally *do this!*"

And his wife would say, "You're crazy!"

Mr. Pink was open to learning more. Maybe the laws really were on tenuous ground, but the only way to know was to start reading up on it. I was gearing up to educate myself the only way I knew how. I would start hanging out in as many dispensaries around town as possible. I would talk to customers. Talk to budtenders. Talk to owners like Jake. I would do my best to analyze their business models as well as I possibly could without getting too nosy. And I would read as much as I could about the legalization movement.

You know those moments when a gust of wind blows through and steals your old life? Those moments when you're forced to dig deep and decide: What am I going to do with the rest of my life?

Call them what you like: moments of growth, of change, of personal development, of enlightenment.

I was right there. I knew if I jumped, the net would appear. I had seen it in my mind's eye.

Marijuana would be my salvation. But only if it was meant to be. Only if it worked for me. Only if it brought joy to me and those around me.

I would work my ass off doing the due diligence.

Something would click, but only if it was aligned with my highest and best self.

I hoped it was.

2

MY EDUCATION

GO AHEAD AND LAUGH, BUT THERE'S ONLY ONE WAY TO research legal marijuana. And I did it. Again and again and again.

Thus began my education. My baptism by fire—er, smoke.

Maybe you've had that experience where you get really into something and then you start seeing it everywhere. You buy yourself that Mini Cooper you've always wanted, and from that day forward, you see nothing but Mini Coopers on the road. "Wow," you think, "they're everywhere!"

Well, I saw medical marijuana everywhere I looked. I took every opportunity I could to check out medical dispensaries in every quarter of Denver. I kept lists of establishments I was going to check out. I bought books about the history and cultivation of marijuana. I'd pick up *High Times*—a magazine I hadn't seen since my teenage years—whenever I saw it on a newsstand. At the time there seemed to be a story about legal marijuana on Denver's TV news every single night. The topic was often a featured story in the *Denver Post*. Marijuana was everywhere.

I was a man on a mission.

What an amazing time it was.

Colorado's medical marijuana laws were rapidly evolving. They'd been first conceived as a way to allow sick patients to grow their own marijuana plants at home. But citizens who needed it the most—such as cancer patients—were too sick to raise finicky plants. So the law was created to license "caregivers"—family, friends, nurses—who could grow marijuana for their intended patients. You could see where this would inevitably lead: Most caregivers didn't have the expertise to grow marijuana. So the Colorado Department of Public Health and the Environment decided to allow the licensing of formal dispensaries—stores that sold product that had been grown by professional growers. If you were sick or in pain, you didn't have to rely on your nephew's brown thumb for your supply. You could just bop into a store and buy some weed from a complete stranger.

The law had transformed a portion of Broadway, in downtown Denver, into a carnival of marijuana dispensaries that locals had dubbed the Green Mile. At least twenty dispensaries dotted this strip of Broadway within a mile of the intersection with Evans Avenue. Neon signs of green crosses and flashing marijuana leaves soon peeked out of many windows.

By law, you could not enter a marijuana dispensary unless you were an employee or a customer with a red card. Inside, you'd find long counters where budtenders proudly displayed glass jars brimming with sticky buds. They'd also sell all the tools you needed: glass pipes, bongs, vaporizers, lighters, you name it. Other ganja-preneurs were making and selling their own edibles—the legendary marijuana brownies, not to mention chocolate bars, suckers, cookies, fudge, hard candies, and gummy bears laden with marijuana. They would bake, cook, or mold them elsewhere and bring them to the dispensaries to be sold to eager customers who clamored for the novelty of it all.

These days, you are prevented by law from lighting up or eating your purchase in dispensaries. The industry firmly adheres to the liquor store model. You buy your product, you get it wrapped in childproof packaging, and you leave the premises to consume it. And no, you cannot consume it right outside the premises or anywhere else in public, nor behind the wheel of your car.

But, hey, this was 2009—the crazy days of medical marijuana's ascendancy. You'd walk into dispensaries to find insanely long lines, and the management's solution to take the edge off the wait was to pass a lighted joint down the line for everyone to enjoy.

I remember from my days running those ice cream shops how wonderful it was to watch people walk out the door with smiles on their faces. They had just bought some of our delicious product, and they were heading out into a warm summer night to enjoy it with their friends and family. For me, that was one of the pleasures of being a retailer. It was hard to observe the same reaction in the world of corporate real estate. But here, watching these folks, it all came back to me. It was beautiful to see people of all walks of life—some of them very obviously ill—partaking in this communal bakefest. It was in these times I saw the calming effect of weed. It brought people together, it was creating unity. I was stunned and was left wondering "Why had this ever been illegal?"

When you got to the head of the line, the budtenders asked the question I'd been hearing all over town. The question that was at once esoteric, mysterious, and frustrating: "So, what kind of weed do you like to smoke?"

By then, I had begun digging into the history and lore of marijuana. I knew that there were three basic species: *Cannabis sativa, Cannabis indica,* and *Cannabis ruderalis.* The sativas, which grow no taller than 6 feet high, are known for impacting one's mind, for conjuring psychedelic highs. The indicas, which can grow in the wild as tall as 25 feet high, impact your body. If you are suffering from physical pain, as so many cancer, AIDS, and glaucoma patients are, indicas are what budtenders are likely to recommend. The ruderalises, which have very low amounts of the psychoactive ingredient tetrahydrocannabinol (THC), are of little use for our purposes but are great for growing hemp—marijuana's hardworking, industrial cousin.

The Green Mile was like a crash course at Marijuana University. The better-organized shops would have twenty-five different types of pots, all with exotic-sounding, evocative names: OG Kush. Bubba Kush. Cheesequake. Grape Cola. Waldo. White Dawg. White Queen. White Rhino. Supernova. Alaskan Thunder Fuck. And these were just the tip of the iceberg.

No one knows how many strains there actually are. Some people have opined that there are as many as five thousand, but the number is probably limited only by the human imagination, much like varieties of roses. These marijuana strains are grown from seeds that had been noticed by humans at least twelve thousand years ago, around the dawn of agriculture, in southern and central Asia. Holy men and women in every ancient culture would have prized the plant as a necessary ingredient in their sacramental toolkit. Its highly aromatic buds could be used for perfumes, medicines, and of course desirable intoxicants.

If ancient humans did not care for cannabis, they wouldn't have bothered to transport the seeds of this indigenous plant from the foothills of the Himalayas to the rest of world. Modern archaeologists have turned up evidence of cannabis at sites that date as far back as eight thousand years ago, in places ranging from China to Romania to India and Egypt and Europe. Once shared, these seeds and their resulting buds flourished throughout the world. The ancestors of the strains I saw in the Colorado dispensaries had been smoked by ancient shamans during religious rites, and their effect had been prized as a way to achieve spiritual transcendence.

Historical figures closer to our time loved the bud, too. Researchers have found pipes in William Shakespeare's garden in England that show evidence of having been used to smoke not tobacco but cannabis. We have to wonder: When Shakespeare sang the praises of "a noted weed" in Sonnet 76, was he thinking of marijuana?

The less psychoactive version of the plant, hemp, has thousands of industrial uses. Its seeds can be eaten as a protein-rich food, its durable stalks can be woven into fabric and paper, and its resins can be pressed into service as lamp oil or ethanol. Mariners fashioned sails and clothing out of its precious fibers. At least three of the American founders—George Washington, John Adams, and Thomas Jefferson—commented on the plant's usefulness in their writings. Washington and Jefferson grew it on their plantations and left us detailed notes on its cultivation. Mind you, there's no evidence that Americans during this period knew or understood the potential of cannabis as a recreational intoxicant. The plant they grew had little THC in it, so unless they had exceptionally experimental personalities, they probably wouldn't have bothered smoking it. The plant the Founding Fathers knew was a low-maintenance cash crop that put money in their pockets.

With tobacco, you cure and smoke the leaf. With cannabis, the object of devotion is the flowering, resinous bud of the female plant. The smell of these buds is heady and intoxicating. Even with the lid of a glass jar clamped shut, you can catch a whiff and start to imagine that you're getting a little high.

Outwardly, all buds look a little alike and a little different. Hold them in your hand, peer at them closely, and you'll see dried strands of the plant's stigmas, the long parts of the plants that aid in pollination. Those parts will look tan, orange, even yellow. Sniff the buds and you'll catch hints of everything from skunk to citrus, fruit punch, spicy cloves, grape, cola, or even lemon meringue pie.

On my first couple of outings to Denver's dispensaries, my naïveté didn't surprise the clerks. They went out of their way to teach me.

"Look," they'd say. "What kind of effect do you want? Do you want some couch lock? After you've smoked, you can't pry your body off the couch, except for the promise of half a bag of Oreos and a gallon of ice-cold milk? Or do you want some dance-your-ass-off-and-talk-all-night weed?"

Wow, I thought. There's a lot to know, and I can see only the tip of the iceberg.

Their coaching quickly veered into the realm of the connoisseur:

Was I looking for a mellow high?

Was I looking to bliss out into that ancient, shamanistic transcendence?

Did I have cancer? Did I want to quell the queasiness of chemotherapy?

Did I want to take the edge off arthritis or fibromyalgia?

Did I want to relieve the pressure in my eyeballs from my glaucoma?

Or—considering I looked healthy—was I just looking to throw a comforting blanket over my old snowboarding injury?

Because, whatever I wanted, there was a marijuana for that.

And if I didn't like any of the marijuana these guys sold, there was always another shop right next door.

With Colorado's red card in my pocket, the idiotic adolescent dance was banished forever. No longer did I have to call around to a buddy . . . who knew a guy who knew a guy. No longer did I have to hide what I was doing. No longer did I have to smoke skanky weed. All I had to do was hit up my ATM and fork over the cash for the prime stuff—good genetics grown with care and brought to market when it was still fresh. In the early days, I could smoke in the shop or in my home. Smoking in public was still frowned on.

All in all, I began to regard my new education as a beautiful yet somehow complex transaction.

If I can compare it to anything, it would be like that moment I talked about earlier, when you're out at a fine restaurant and the sommelier arrives at your table to talk about wine. The second she speaks, she is initiating you into a specialized language honed over centuries to describe the seemingly indescribable—notes, nose, legs, palate, mouthfeel . . .

You know these words. If you're a reasonably educated person of a certain socioeconomic strata, words like these have undoubtedly entered your lexicon. Depending on the breadth of your connoisseurship, you might have trained your senses to notice and then talk about similar attributes of fine cigars, dark chocolate, and olive oil.

Marijuana, I was beginning to see, was like that—only more obviously so.

When you're buying wine, for example, you don't factor how drunk you're going to get into the equation. That's because all wines have about the same potency. Perhaps a better analogy for marijuana is the experience of walking into a microbrewery, where the chalkboard lists beers and their alcohol content. A visitor to these premises quickly picks up on the subtleties as she sips her way through a sample flight. "Oh," she thinks, "this lager is only 4.5 percent, but this 'high-gravity' bourbon stout is a brain-blowing 11 percent alcohol. Oh yeah—I can taste the alcohol."

The interesting thing about marijuana, I was learning, was that the spectrum of intoxication was wider and growing every day.

Back in 1969, the kids who toked at the famous Woodstock Festival in upstate New York got high on marijuana that was a mere 3 percent THC. Considering how legendary Woodstock has become, you might think 3 percent is a lot. But today in the United States, commercial growers are cultivating numerous strains of marijuana that have been clocked at 23 percent THC or higher. That's a sevenfold increase over the weed that baked Woodstock.

It's nice to remember the old days, but I could not legitimately call myself a marijuana connoisseur until I'd dipped into these headier waters.

Why is the THC percentage increasing? The upswing actually has a lot to do with the time-honored tradition of breeding plants and animals to enhance certain aspects of each. Breeders around the world are obsessed with pushing the limits. They think it's cool to breed increasingly stronger strains. "Okay, that was good," they'd say, "but how can we top what we just did?" They were dedicated to working with the various male and female plants, breeding them together, and testing the result working to get the "best"—this was *their* paint, brush, and canvas.

The new generation of legal American growers truly is unparalleled in this respect. For example, the Netherlands is renowned for its liberal marijuana policies. Weed is technically illegal in the Netherlands, but the state follows a blind-eye policy of tolerance. As a result, the Dutch are among the most educated growers of marijuana in the world. And yet the average THC sold in Amsterdam's cannabis cafés is only 13.5 percent, according to a 2013 report. That's several percentage points lower than some of the heavy-hitting strains I was finding as I prowled around downtown Denver.

At first glance, breeding plants with higher THC sounds awesome, but I could already see that high-THC marijuana would leave the nascent cannabis industry vulnerable to criticism if it did not take pains to explain to customers what they were buying. If retailers did not produce consistently potent products and educate their customers in a way that was meaningful to the customers and enabled them to make informed decisions, the states would step in and force them to do so. Most of the budtenders and dispensary owners I was meeting were conscientious on that score. They took extravagant pains to educate consumers as much as possible before they parted with their cash and went home to enjoy their weed.

It made good business sense. They didn't want people to try a strain that was so strong of an intoxicant that they would never come back. For the sake of the industry, they wanted everyone's visit to a cannabis shop to be as delicious as the memories of the ice cream shops that I still carried in my heart.

SO WHAT HAPPENED? How did a plant that intoxicated ancient shamans, inspired Shakespeare, and enriched Thomas Jefferson end up so reviled and banished from modern American history?

The books I was reading told a fascinating story.

I think it's fair to say that the origins of American marijuana prohibition have their roots in the ugly side of human nature—racism and greed. As late as the nineteenth century, when cowboys roamed the West and horses and railroads were the only way to cross the country, cannabis was openly grown and used medicinally. Farmers still grew the low-THC hemp variety that Jefferson had grown. But a number of doctors and folk medicine practitioners had begun realizing the plant's medical potential. When doctors prescribed it, druggists dispensed it to patients under the name *Cannabis indica*. In fact, you can still find antique medicine bottles referencing this ingredient on the faded, yellowing labels. Newbie collectors often pay too much for those bottles, assuming that they're a rarity. In fact, say the experts, the bottles are not that rare at all. Cannabis was once prescribed with about the same frequency as aspirin.

But by 1913, Americans started to pass laws against a substance they called "marihuana." The fact that these laws were passed in the American Southwest—in Colorado, Nevada, Texas, Utah, Wyoming, and as far west as California—should give us a hint what was going on: Mexican laborers were flocking to seek work in these areas, which had once been—how quickly we forget—their customary stomping grounds in old Mexico. On their off hours, to blow off steam, they smoked weed.

I don't think I'm stretching history by saying that white Americans of that time were wary of foreigners, as they saw them though their "manifest destiny" goggles, and they didn't much care for these immigrants' "locoweed."

When newspapers of the day wrote about this bizarre "new" drug that Mexicans smoked—a weed, it was said, that drove Mexicans insane, imbued them with "superhuman strength," and "turned them into bloodthirsty murderers"—the reporters conveniently avoided using words Americans would understand, such as *hemp* or *cannabis*. Instead, they printed the unfamiliar, foreign-sounding *marihuana*. If they had used the King's English, I'm pretty sure that our great-grandparents and great-great-grandparents would have called bullshit on the burgeoning anti-marijuana campaign and saved our generation a lot of work.

In 1930, the U.S. Congress formed the Federal Bureau of Narcotics (called the FBN) and appointed the nation's first drug czar, Harry J. Anslinger, a dour-faced Pennsylvanian who became renowned throughout the nation for his crusade against marijuana. He would singlehandedly direct U.S. drug policy until 1962.

Modern Americans would, and should, find his tactics atrocious. He launched a powerful media campaign to educate Americans about the dangers of marijuana, linking the plant's use not only to Mexicans but also African Americans, and warned that users of the drug would be driven to acts of rape and violence against white women. What an abhorrent claim to make.

I don't know where he got his information. It's quite likely that the salacious stories he trotted out to the press from his now-infamous "Gore File" were spun out of whole cloth. But they worked. By 1935, two years after Prohibition ended, most of the states in the United States had passed laws against marijuana, and by 1937, President Franklin D. Roosevelt was signing the Marihuana Tax Act into law. Congress had debated all of three and a half months on this bill, which didn't seek to ban cannabis outright. It sought to levy such a high tax on it that it would be safely out of the public's reach. There was only one naysayer to the bill, a medical doctor from the American Medical Association, who testified that the government had not proved its case.

Where was the scientific evidence that showed marijuana was indeed as bad as the FBN had portrayed it? the good doctor asked.

The congressional committee that heard his testimony derided him soundly. After all, everyone knew "marihuana" was evil. Why get hung up on silly things such as scientific proof?

Around the same time, a low-budget B-movie called *Tell Your Children* was making the rounds of the bijous on Main Streets all across America. This was the film that would later be retitled *Reefer Madness*. It purports to tell the story of what happens when small-time marijuana dealers corrupt young innocent white kids from a typical American high school. Throughout the film, these young people are lured to parties where they are unwittingly offered marijuana cigarettes, with terrifying results. Mary, a virginal teenager, is shot dead during a marijuana-fueled argument, and her innocent boyfriend, Bill, is framed into believing he killed her while under the influence. Ralph, another young man who knows the truth, becomes consumed with guilt and increasingly marijuana-paranoid as Bill's murder trial proceeds. In one absurd scene, Ralph urges a friend to play her piano faster, as if his drug-addled mind can be calmed only by the cacophonous clanking. By the end of the movie, two people have been violently murdered, one marijuana dealer-user leaps to her death out of an open window, Mary's brother runs over a pedestrian with his car, and paranoid Ralph is sentenced to an institution for the criminally insane.

Speaking as a modern American moviegoer, *Reefer Madness* is hilarious, one of those movies that's so bad it's good. The movie poster is so lurid and over the top that we have hung a copy in one of our dispensaries. But the audiences who saw *Reefer Madness* in the 1930s must have been horrified. The whole film is designed to show that marijuana causes everything from insanity to murder to uncontrollable sexuality.

With *Reefer Madness* in the theaters and a new anti-marijuana law on the books, you'd think Americans would steer clear of weed forever.

Yeah, right.

In 1942, at the height of World War II, the United States was facing a shortage of materials. The government produced a short propaganda film entitled *Hemp for Victory*, urging farmers to grow hemp, which could be used to make valuable fibers, rope, and fabric for the war effort. I'm sure that the irony of this situation was lost on those who authorized the film and the agricultural agencies that subsequently cleared hundreds of thousands of acres of farmland for wartime hemp planting, but it's not lost on us. Because the government had neatly eradicated hemp from the nation's fields, it was now obliged to reeducate a new generation of farmers about what hemp was. By the way, for decades after, the government would deny that this sixteen-minute film had ever been made. Had marijuana activists not found and distributed bootleg copies, the film would have disappeared from American culture altogether.

Then came the 1960s, that tie-dyed decade that sparked so much change in America. It seemed that every young person in the country was getting high—and arrested. In response, the government locked down marijuana again, this time classifying it as a Schedule I drug, along with heroin and LSD. Schedule I drugs theoretically have no redeeming medical value and a high potential for abuse. (This classification still stands today.) But since so many otherwise law-abiding teens—read: white teens—were getting busted for marijuana, Congress probably felt compelled to research marijuana's true impact, so it punted that task to a committee for investigation. Two years later, in 1972, that commission—much to its credit, considering the politically charged atmosphere surrounding drugs in the Vietnam years—announced that it found no reason to enact strong laws for marijuana. Some points the commission made:

- "[C]annabis does not lead to physical dependence."
- "The overwhelming majority of marihuana users do not progress to other drugs."
- No "substantial evidence existed of a causal connection between the use of marihuana and the commission of violent or aggressive acts."
- "[M]arihuana was usually found to inhibit the expression of aggressive impulses by pacifying the user."

Basically, the commission said what every marijuana activist has tried to say since: The drug wasn't addictive, or a gateway drug, or an instigator of violence. If anything, it mellowed people out and caused them to relax.

As I was learning now, there is little evidence to support the oft-touted gateway drug hypothesis, even today. Yes, some Americans do indeed move on to harder drugs, but the vast majority do not. Marijuana is the world's most popular illicit drug, and certainly the most popular in the United States, but once you move beyond marijuana, the statistics show that use of heavier drugs quickly declines rapidly. Marijuana has tempted four out of ten Americans. About 15 percent of Americans have tried cocaine; fewer still have tried crack or heroin. I'll bet you know tons of people—friends, acquaintances, family members, perhaps even yourself—who have used marijuana without ever switching to stronger drugs. Interestingly, in the Netherlands, the statistics are even more striking. The Dutch found that when they permitted marijuana sales in private cafés—effectively taking marijuana out of the hands of street drug dealers and giving it to the baristas—the rate at which Dutch citizens moved to harder drugs like cocaine and heroin dropped markedly. The percentage of Dutch folks who have tried cocaine is 2 percent, as compared to about 15 percent in the United States. I daresay that there is nothing intrinsic to the marijuana plant that forces its users to crave more dangerous highs. If marijuana is a gateway drug, then so are caffeine, alcohol, and tobacco. The real issue probably has something to do with how often marijuana users hang out with street dealers of hard illicit drugs.

Back in the 1970s, the National Commission on Marihuana and Drug Abuse recommended *decriminalizing* the drug. If the federal government wanted to set a reasonable precedent for the states, then perhaps users could be hit with a nominal fine.

Such a permissive policy did not sit well with President Richard M. Nixon, arguably the twitchiest fellow ever to hold that office. Nixon ignored every point in the commission's report and made marijuana the top priority for his new creation—the Drug Enforcement Agency (DEA). Thanks to Nixon, every one of the bullet points in the commission's report would be systematically ignored, distorted, and perverted to serve the agency's own goals.

By the time I was growing up in the 1970s and 1980s, kids like me were being taught by school nurses and visiting cops that marijuana was a gateway drug. Anyone you asked told you that marijuana would kill infants in the womb, shrink a boy's testicles, blot out your intelligence, and lead inevitably to cocaine, heroin, murder, and madness.

It was as if we had returned to the days of *Reefer Madness*.

Only later, when I was older and thinking about investing in marijuana as a business, did I learn how some very powerful people were suspected of having manipulated marijuana laws for their own benefit. After all, if marijuana was dangerous, then bureaucrats like Harry Anslinger were guaranteed government jobs for life. If marijuana was illegal, then law enforcement agencies had a new weapon for crushing those they regarded as undesirables—whether they were Mexicans, African Americans, or hippies. If marijuana had no medical use, then the burgeoning medical lobby could neatly eradicate a cheap folk medicine from the American pharmacopoeia, paving the way for costly, lab-designed drugs. Media moguls such as William Randolph Hearst had a demon drug that would sell newspapers. And industry titans such as John D. Rockefeller, Andrew Mellon, and a host of other industrial manufacturers of the world could effectively wipe out hemp products—natural rope, fuel, fibers—from the American marketplace, leaving a void that would be taken over by products that could be sourced from their own petroleum-based products: nylon, gasoline, and oil. Huge lumber companies would provide wood from old-growth forests to create the kinds of products that the more sustainable plant, hemp, had once been used to manufacture.

This is the dark side of the anti-marijuana story. You'll find it all in the history books, if you know where to look, but to breathe it today in mixed political company is enough to get you branded as a conspiracy theorist, or worse.

MY TUTELAGE IN THE WORLD of marijuana has never ended, and I learn more every day. The more I learned, I could see, too, that the business was promising but in dire need of optimization.

One thing I noticed right away was that most of the growers and dispensary owners I was meeting were marijuana lovers first and businesspeople second. This is highly typical in almost any small business. People think, "I like making leather goods—I'll open a leather shop." "I like books—I'll open a bookshop." "I'm a foodie with capital—let me open the restaurant of my dreams."

And yeah, you can do that, but 50 percent of all businesses fail in the first two years, if not sooner, usually because the owner has enthusiasm and expertise in one area alone—and it's not making money.

Unfortunately, I was meeting many people who believed that all they had to do to make a killing in cannabis was rent a storefront, put out a bunch of glass jars full of weed, and start hawking their wares to their friends.

To quote one: "All you need is a table and a bucket to sell weed."

Some of these newcomers were rich kids who had the family money to set themselves up in a shop. Some were street dealers who were looking to go legit after a lifetime of criminal activity. Some had such a bare-bones approach to business that they leaped into the industry with nothing more than $10,000 in cash, a cheap sign, and a table.

What they lacked was the vision to see what this industry would become in the long term: America's newest consumer product. Its packaging, marketing, the public's perception, and its brand would all impact one's success.

Some people saw it, but most did not. Aside from the pang of munchies, they weren't all that hungry to grow to the next level. They weren't setting up their businesses efficiently. And they lacked a competitive drive.

As much as I enjoy marijuana, I love creating even more. Creating the vision I saw in my mind's eye would become an adventure from which I could not extricate myself. I didn't want to; I was falling in love.

I was also beginning to understand that growing marijuana was labor-intensive and costly. Nearly all marijuana in the United States—legal or otherwise—is grown indoors. (There are a few notable exceptions, such as California's Golden Triangle.) The early hippies grew indoors to evade the authorities, so the current wisdom on the subject is that marijuana is best grown indoors because you can control its environment and inputs. That's why it costs commercial growers like Jake as much as it does to grow one pound of usable marijuana.

Early on, as I went around town I was occasionally invited to visit other people's indoor warehouses—what people in the business simply call "grows"—it occurred to me that there had to be a better way. But I was still too new to the business to try anything risky. I just needed to get into the business. I'd start small. I'd grow indoors. I'd learn the business from the ground up and then learn ways to innovate.

I also needed some venture capital. I had little of my own that I could sink into the business. I would need more.

My wife thought I was crazy. We had always been cut from a different cloth in that respect. She had an excellent job as a sports marketing executive. America's professional sports teams were lucky to have her pulling for them, believe me. But despite everything she'd seen me accomplish in my previous companies, she still believed that a career was all about landing a killer job. Her resistance to my legal marijuana concept eventually went from gentle to aggressive.

It didn't help that one day one of my daughters innocently inquired, "Daddy, why do you smell like lemons all the time?"

My first rule of parenting is never lie to your kids. So I sat all three of them down and told them all that I was thinking about entering the legal marijuana business. We talked about what marijuana was and why grown-ups would want to buy it. The different odors they smelled on my clothes—lemons, yes, but also pine, skunk, mango, blueberry, and so on—came from the plants I was spending so much time with. Basically, I patiently answered every single question they had until the questions dried up and they got bored of talking about how their daddy spent his day.

My wife had a lot of fears.

You have three daughters.

What if you end up arrested?

What if you end up bankrupt again?

And on and on.

Over the next four years, her worries only grew, even after the money started to flow.

On the other end of the spectrum were people like my mom. She had some concerns about my new venture, but she always wanted to know more, to understand. She was open to the possibility that if the state said marijuana was legal, maybe, just maybe, this could be a huge opportunity.

When I wanted an open mind to bounce ideas off of, I went to talk to Mr. Pink. Most of the neighborhood congregated at his swimming pool during our off hours. His parties were some of my favorite memories, brimming with interesting people, camaraderie, and joy.

He and I would also meet for drinks at the Tavern Lowry in Denver and kick ideas around.

We saw eye to eye on a lot of things. You could tell by the questions he asked.

How much money do you think a start-up would cost?

What will you spend it on?

What would be the return?

How will you distribute?

What were strengths, weaknesses, opportunities, and threats of the business?

From the beginning, both of us grasped that the key to success in this business was growing the marijuana. By law, we were not yet required to be vertically integrated—that would come soon. But I knew the business model would work better if we were vertically integrated. We would then control not only the supply and the quality of the marijuana but also the packaging, branding, and point-of-sale marketing.

The biggest unknown, everyone thought, was that somehow the federal government would one day grow weary of the states legalizing marijuana, then descend on us all, seize our businesses and facilities, shut us down, arrest us, and hit us all with federal charges. That was definitely a worst-case scenario. It was a consideration, but it was extreme. I preferred to look on the bright side.

Landlords aren't going to be eager to have you rent from them, Mr. Pink said. You're looking at higher rent to make up for their risk. And the insurance will be higher too, I surmised.

The illegal drug business would not go away. Even in Denver I knew marijuana users who refused to get their legal red cards; they just didn't trust the system. They preferred to drive to their buddy's house and buy their weed the old-fashioned way, even if they had to patronize known drug dealers to do so.

Mr. Pink listened.

Whenever we talked about this at his home, his wife would be half listening to our discussion. She looked at me as if I were nuts. "Even if the state has voted for it, it's against federal law," she would say.

"I'm just listening," her husband said. And then he added absently, "That's the thing—it's not illegal anymore . . ."

"It's not," I echoed.

We talked about it a few times, just kicking the idea around. Mr. Pink would get so passionate about the possibilities. Our conversations still ended with him saying *"We should do this!"*

One week, I promised to meet him at the Tavern Lowry so we could talk over some of the numbers I had pulled together. Mr. Pink was already there when I arrived. I walked in with a spreadsheet I'd generated and laid it facedown on the table in front of me. We slowly gravitated from small talk to talking about the business. I ran through the numbers from memory, never deigning to flip over the spreadsheet. This is why I like business guys, or guys like Mr. Pink who spend their lives thinking about numbers. Mr. Pink could see that if what I was telling him was true, we could see a profit in six to twelve months. And we'd have the advantage of throwing ourselves into a business that was utterly, wonderfully new. That probably doesn't seem like a big deal, but it is. The rarest thing in the world is the growth industry. Some people know just how to maximize its potential. Other people sabotage their own chances of success.

"I want in," he said suddenly. "If you put in the time, I could see putting in some of the money."

We shook on it. Mr. Pink had to get going. It wasn't until he'd left that I realized that I'd never shown him my spreadsheet. It was as if the real numbers hadn't mattered. He trusted me enough to see where we were going.

A few days later, Mr. Pink opened a business checking account at a bank where he had some connections. And then proceeded to wire in $125,000.

We were unlike any of the other ganjapreneurs I had met. The former treasury agent and the tall, square-jawed businessman.

Congrats to us. We were drug dealers.

3

FIRST GROW,
FIRST BLOOD

MY WEED WASN'T GOING TO GROW ITSELF.

I needed a grower. An expert. A master. Someone who could hit the ground running, help me buy and install equipment, and see me safely through my first harvest. Hopefully, this person would like working for me and want to stay on. He or she would want to grow with the business.

I needed expertise. Desperately. If you forced me to tell you all I knew about plants, I'd probably opine that plants came from seeds. You stuck a seed in dirt and watered it, and *voila!*—before you knew it, you had anything from a houseplant to a 50-foot banana tree growing out of your little clay pot. Hell, my front lawn was made of tiny little plants. I watered my lawn, and it grew and stayed green. How different could *that* grass be from the grass you smoked? I had no idea. I didn't take care of my lawn. Landscapers did.

So basically, I was clueless about the world of plants.

But I was *not* a stranger to hiring people. I'd done it before, countless times, for all my other companies. At my last firm, I had a person who screened applicants for us and flagged ones that merited a look.

Somehow, though, I didn't think a corporate headhunter was going to be of much help in *this* talent search. So one morning after breakfast I sat at my computer and cranked out a want ad that I planned to upload to Denver's Craigslist.

MASTER GROWER FOR MEDICAL MARIJUANA CAREGIVER NEEDED

I talked about the kind of business I was hoping to start, the kind of person I was looking for, and asked for respondents' experience and salary requirements.

Then I hit send.

The ad wormed its way into the world, took root in the world of the Internet, and in a few hours responses started bouncing back to my inbox.

I don't have to tell you what the Web is like. Some of the applications I received were well meaning and earnest but painfully illiterate. Some people were out-of-towners who had heard about Colorado's marijuana Green Rush and were eager to quit their jobs back home for a chance to get their foot in the door. Some openly admitted that they were not master growers, but they were willing to do anything to be involved in such an enterprise. One applicant told me he had tons of experience, but he'd recently spoken with his attorney, who advised him that he probably should only affiliate himself with a "legal, legitimate" business. (Good advice.) Another writer said he was hesitant to give me his resume, because, well, he had never had to do that before. He and several other applicants admitted that they'd been growing illegally for years and it was just a little weird to be talking about this via the Internet.

I got a few crackpots. Some treated me as if I'd dared to penetrate the hallowed world of marijuana geekdom that should only be trod by other longtime growers. If I was looking to *hire* a grower, then I was clearly not one of the initiated, and so why would anyone want to bother with me? One e-mail message became progressively more belligerent as it waxed on in this vein. My correspondent closed by saying that I should not even think of tracing his IP address. He had blocked it with sophisticated technology.

Amid the hits and misses were reasonable, articulate folks who seemed like the sort I'd be interested in talking to. But even they had reached out to me with aliases and stubbornly refused to share their phone numbers.

Great, I thought. It's just my luck to be recruiting in a community of people who wanted to be hired but didn't want to reveal their identities. It was a slog getting them to phone me back. The ones I spoke to this way over the phone were exceedingly wary.

"Um, why do you want to hire a grower?" was a frequent question I got.

I'd explain that I was looking to enter the legal medical marijuana business in a big way. Mr. Pink and I were currently in the process of signing up every patient we could. Back then, all a medical marijuana patient needed to do was list our names as their caregivers on their application. We were offering every friend or family member we knew the opportunity to get their red card and asked them to assign us as their caregiver.

We were banking on a few things. We assumed that there were quite a few people in our social circle who already smoked and who routinely got their weed off the street. It would be no trouble to convert these people to our business. Why go through the hassle of patronizing an unsavory business when you could buy from a legit one? We also assumed that we knew lots of law-abiding people who had smoked in the past but who had never pursued marijuana beyond that adolescent phase because they were too nervous to deal with drug dealers. And we thought there were probably lots of people who were curious about marijuana but had never tried it for the same reason: They didn't want to break the law.

Years later, I'd have to say that these three demographics still accurately describe the types of people we see in our dispensaries:

current users, past users, curious never users. Well, our hunch was correct. We would ultimately enroll about three hundred patients. That told us that we were legally permitted by law to grow up to 1,800 marijuana plants. We would sell the product of that many plants to various dispensaries, theoretically satisfying the needs of our clients.

Typically, as soon as I explained all this, the conversation with prospective growers/employees would peter out. My callers didn't quite know what to ask. And then I found myself having to sell *them* on the opportunity.

"I think this could be a good job for someone who's thinking of going legit," I said. "Who wants the hassle of funding their own operation?"

"Uh-huh."

"So, what do you think?"

"Um, I dunno."

Most of these calls went nowhere. I could hear the disembodied voices fading away over the phone. My sixth sense told me something was up. Was my frankness spooking people? Were marijuana growers so used to avoiding authority figures that they were essentially incapable of socially normal behavior?

I offered to meet my best candidates at a sandwich shop on Hampden in south Denver. It was near my home and central to Denver, easy to get to. I'd go down there to meet potential candidates in this comfortable space with black-and-white photos on the textured walls and wait for job seekers who never arrived. Maybe some of them peeked in, caught a glimpse of a six-foot-three, sandy-haired, clean-cut guy waiting for them at the back of the room, and immediately figured I was a cop.

I met three people in the sandwich shop, but none impressed me. They seemed too frenetic, too antsy, as if they thought this job possibility was just too good to be true and any moment the cops would bust in. One was a nice young man, twenty-seven years old, who had just finished eight years in prison for growing in his home. He was busted one month before he was about to start college. He never got to go; instead he spent twice the normal span of college years in a federal prison because he'd done what I was working so hard to get into.

One day as I was waiting, in walked a man in his early thirties. He was about two doughnuts away from being perfectly round, and as he shuffled up to meet me, he was hiking up his pants.

"You Chris?" he said.

"Yeah, that's me."

"I responded to your ad on Craigslist. I'm Adam."

We sat. We talked. Adam struck me as a kind of passionate, Zen-like sloth. His movements were slow and deliberate, and when I asked him a question, his eyes would mull over the words and rove around the room as he gave it thoughtful consideration. Unlike the other people I'd met, he wasn't worried about a thing. He was calm as hell.

"How long have you been growing?" I asked.

"Fifteen years."

That didn't compute. "Wait—how old are you again?"

"Thirty-one."

"And you've been growing how long?"

"Fifteen years."

"That means you've been growing since you were sixteen years old. How is that possible?"

He smiled. It turned out that he'd grown up in California, the son of a couple of hippies who grew weed for themselves every summer. He had helped his parents on and off over the years, then got into it on his own at age sixteen.

Mostly he was into welding, and dreamed of building for himself an underground grow facility out of old shipping containers. A place where he could disappear from the cares of the world and commune with his most excellent buds. That seemed a little extreme to me, but I would soon learn that some of the best growers were genuine oddballs. Right then, the most important thing about Adam was that he'd been growing marijuana nearly half his life.

I'd found my grower.

MY GOOD FRIEND DAX had been working hard to find suitable space for our grow operation. He had pulled some strings around town with other real estate broker friends of his who knew of commercial buildings for rent. He had helped me to locate a warehouse space that was just under 5,000 square feet.

Now, this was 2009, and most of the landlords around town were still reeling from the collapse of the housing bubble. A lot of businesses had gone under, and a lot of people had lost their shirts. The word around town was that landlords were desperate to lock in new tenants with long-term leases.

Well, apparently they weren't desperate enough to lock in *me*.

The going rate for warehouse space was about $4 a square foot. But when we started approaching people, we found that all these spaces could be ours for a mere $12 a square foot.

In a "desperate" economy, landlords were perfectly happy to charge legal marijuana growers almost three times the going rate.

I had expected this. I wasn't surprised. That didn't mean I wasn't feeling bent about having to pay such a premium. Privately I started calling that premium "the vig," which, in the criminal world, is the interest paid to a loan shark. In my world, the vig was the amount a legal cannabis grower paid above the going rate to get people with whom he did business comfortable with the risk of our industry.

Landlords accept a risk when they take on new tenants. They want someone who's going to be able to pay the rent on time for the length of the lease. If a tenant defaults, the landlord loses time finding another tenant. If a landlord has to retrofit the building, or undo what the last tenant has left behind in his wake, then the landlord might actually be deeper in the hole than he or she originally was.

There wasn't a landlord in town who knew what to make of the legal marijuana business. Yes, they'd heard it was now legal to grow and sell this product, but everyone was aware that it was still federally illegal. What if the state law was repealed and the feds seized these commercial rental properties? To protect themselves, landlords *had* to charge more.

At least, that's how they saw it.

I had signed a lease on a handsome property on South Platte River Drive. You unlocked a street-facing gate and entered a nice courtyard trimmed with shrubs and about a dozen trees. This low-key elegance was costing me about $5,000 a month.

Inside, the space had been subdivided with walls, windows, and doors in a way that had made sense when it was built. Since I was completely ignorant about my new business, I thought I would try to fit my grow into the existing spaces. History would later show that I should have demolished all the existing walls and finishes and rebuilt the whole place to suit my specific purposes.

"We have to produce a good harvest," I told Adam as we walked through the space, our voices echoing in the darkness.

"No problem. We'll be up and running in no time."

Easier said than done. In the great outdoors, Mother Nature takes care of everything. A seed falls on open soil, water gets the seed growing, and a tiny plant begins to grow. In its lifetime, that plant will need sunlight, water, and air (carbon dioxide) to grow. Marijuana likes full sun, and while it will grow when it's exceedingly hot, it really prefers temperatures to stay between 77 and 85 degrees Fahrenheit. It does well in humid environments, but it doesn't really like when humidity climbs above 55 percent.

Living outdoors may seem like paradise for a plant, but it's also highly unpredictable. You never know when a predator or a thoughtless galumphing animal is going to tramp through your crop and crush it to the ground. You could have six weeks of great rain, then nothing. Temperatures and humidity fluctuate constantly, putting our plant's life in peril.

So it's really no wonder that so many of the world's commercial crops are grown indoors, in greenhouses, where their human caretakers can control every aspect of the plant's life, from seed to harvest.

But since marijuana is probably the world's most maligned and targeted plant, it's safe to say that for the last seventy years in the United States, it's been grown largely indoors in cinder-block spaces not unlike the one I'd just rented. If you're growing an illegal substance, your risk of being detected by law enforcement will increase dramatically the more you put your plants on view. All American "experts" on marijuana cultivation were outlaws before the state laws started to change, and they mostly grew indoors.

I wasn't married to the idea of growing my precious harvest in a giant cement box, but all the current wisdom on the subject said this was the only way to go. So I stood by and started writing checks as Adam went to work, subdividing a room within the warehouse into four smaller spaces each with four 1,000-watt high-pressure sodium lights and a wall-mounted air conditioner in each room.

I was surprised, maybe even shocked, to see what a resource-heavy crop indoor-grown marijuana really was. One requirement for plant growth quickly demanded another. First you start with the given that plants need light. So you install powerful lamps that deliver 3,500 foot-candles of light, which sometimes feels like enough light to illuminate every business on the average American Main Street. But powerful grow lamps produce not only light but also heat. Too much heat is bad because it starts to raise the temperature of your grow room. As plants heat up, they transpire, releasing moisture from the minuscule openings in their leaves called stomata. Now your grow room is both too hot and too humid, which marijuana plants don't like. To reduce the temperature and dry up the air, you install air conditioners, which suck that much more power from your local grid.

One power-suck inevitably leads to another power-suck.

Growing marijuana this way is like driving your grandpa's gas-guzzling Chevy Bel Air from the 1950s. It's a sweet ride, but you're paying through the nose to get anywhere.

But there was an upside. If we calibrated all these factors just right, we could manipulate the plants to grow exceedingly well. Instead of starting every plant from seed, we could start a "mother" plant and take cuttings from that plant. When we dipped each cutting in a rooting hormone and stuck it in some growing medium, each cutting would sprout roots and grow into healthy clones of the mother plant. Clones saved us time; we didn't have to wait to grow from seed. From clone to harvest was still a good thirteen weeks, but we could stagger our crops in such a way that every few weeks or so we were harvesting something.

It was a humbling experience for me, seeing those first few plants poke their heads out of the soil and reach toward the lights. Seed-grown or clone, plants grown in this manner were utterly dependent on the care of humans for their survival, but they stubbornly stuck to their own clock. They would not be rushed.

That was a lesson I had to learn, because so much of my life had been about trying to do things quickly. In college, I could cram for exams if I needed to. Stay up all night reviewing the notes I'd taken all semester in class, walk into the exam room at 8:30 the next morning, regurgitate everything onto paper—and ace the test. In my business life, I could cram for a presentation if needed. I'd walk into a room and nail the meeting because I had stuffed every factoid needed into my skull, and I could do it quickly.

Humans are good at cramming. Good at speeding things up. Forcing things to happen ahead of schedule to hit some arbitrary target. Americans, in particular, are experts at this.

But plants don't cram. Within certain parameters, they stick to the clock nature has imprinted on their genes. Like it or not, bro—the plant's schedule was its own, and nothing we could do would speed it up.

But there were things we could do to shape them, nurture them, nudge them to do what we wanted them to do. Every day I'd go to the grow to watch Adam work. If he wasn't building a lamp bracket or fixing some piece of equipment that had gone on the fritz, he liked to talk to the plants and stroke them as he pruned off their excess leaves. By pruning, he was not-so-subtly instructing the plant to put all its resources into growing fat, healthy flower buds.

I'd pick one of those fan leaves off from time to time and inspect it carefully. When I was a boy, I'd see images of the marijuana leaf emblazoned on posters and record albums and T-shirts and human skin. Artists poured their hearts and souls into creating works of art in honor of this ancient plant. Even today there's a whole subculture devoted to marijuana leaf imagery on everything from key chains and socks to women's undergarments. This stuff is all great fun, until you come eye to eye with a real marijuana plant. That's when you realize that the true artistry is Nature's alone. A single leaf typically sprouts five, seven, nine, or thirteen smaller leaflets—mostly odd numbers—and depending on the strain, those leaflets will have slightly serrated or more pronounced serrated edges. They're a rich, glossy green, and handsome in a way that other plants from which humans draw sustenance—corn, wheat, sugarcane—are not.

Wow, I'd think, they are so beautiful.

Sometimes I'd think back to the teenager I once was and how we made such a big deal about scoring some weed on a Friday or Saturday night. Those tortuous, furtive adventures paled in comparison to this. I was now standing in a room surrounded by more marijuana than I'd ever seen in one time or place in my entire life, and it didn't feel wrong, or dirty, or illegal. It felt wonderful. I was standing in my own private garden. Yes, the lights were humming. Yes, I was ensconced in the belly of a cinder-block building. But still, the out-side noise of traffic, the grind of the everyday, the artificial world of business, was blotted out.

For the first time in my professional life, I was aligned with Na-ture, something I had always longed for. These plants were part of Nature. We were taking care of them, and they in turn would take care of us in what was ultimately a beautiful, mysterious transaction between two living things.

Of course, being humans, it was probably inevitable that we would fuck it up.

IN LATE FALL 2009, I was marching happily down the Green Mile in downtown Denver. The large black nylon duffel bag on my shoul-der was emblazoned with the logo of the professional sporting team that had given it to my wife as a gift. Inside the bag I had about three pounds of weed in large Ziploc bags, my first official harvest. We'd grown thirteen different strains with names like Dutch Treat, Lemon Skunk, Northern Lights, Bubblegum, Chronic, AK-47, and more, and I was eager to share them with the world.

I admit that I was a little giddy about the whole thing. My first harvest! Awesome. I had brought these living things into the world. The harvest was small, but I was a player in the burgeoning mari-juana market. But now, as I wound my way through a few of the dispensaries on the Green Mile, I was getting only so-so feedback from potential buyers.

They're nice, but they're not great. Come back when you have some-thing else.

No, but thanks for thinking of us.

Bring something different if you ever come back, okay?

I squelched my pride and listened carefully to the feedback. We hadn't dried the buds long enough. We hadn't trimmed them tightly enough; they still had bits of leaves sticking to them. As a result, they didn't present well. Despite what I was hearing, a few people did make me offers on what I was selling. In fact, I sold all of my harvest before reaching the end of the Green Mile.

That was good *and* bad.

Although what I'd grown wasn't ideal, people still liked it enough to buy. I just didn't have enough of it. Consequently, I wasn't earning nearly enough money to cover my operating costs, and I was far from being able to make good on Mr. Pink's investment.

Now, granted, new businesses plan for this. You don't expect to hit it out of the park on the first round. That's why your start-up costs allow for a few months of low or nonexistent earnings. But still—the clock was ticking. Mr. Pink's money was not going to float us forever. When was I going to see some fat profits?

Looking back, I can see that the handwriting was on the wall the whole time. I was just too blind to see it.

Entrepreneurs are fond of talking about the mistakes businesses make. One of the classics is the business that grew too fast. Its owners pump too much of their capital into growth, the organization doesn't know how to absorb the new paradigm, the system becomes top-heavy and then crumbles. But there is also the phenomenon of not sizing your start-up appropriately. In our case, starting out small wasn't our only problem. We started out small, inefficient, naive, and paranoid.

Adam and I were both naive. As the boss, I should have known to ask better questions. Show me a sample of your weed, for starters. But there were others: What's the biggest grow you've ever run? How would you size a facility to grow 1,800 plants? What would you do differently when dealing with so many plants?

We were sizing ourselves out of the market from the very beginning. For example, a modern, state-of-the-art indoor grow does indeed divide its space into smaller rooms, but not as small as Adam had done. And because we had simply moved into those existing rooms in our facility, we hadn't started a large grow per se but several very small grows. That was a huge mistake out of the gate.

Instead of hiring an electrician to come install a new electrical system that would allow us to switch on the lights and equipment in each room from a central box, we relied on Adam's labyrinthine system of running cheap lights and extension cords connected to lightweight consumer lighting timers. Our electrical outlets looked like the ones fire departments warn everyone about at Christmas time, when foolish people stuff eighteen plugs into the same outlet to keep their holiday decorations going.

Because we were doing things cheap and small-minded, we had unwittingly introduced glaring inefficiencies into the system. Four small grow rooms meant needing four different air conditioners, each running at the same time. Had we designed the warehouse to have one large grow room, we could have gotten by using the one large, efficient AC unit already situated on the roof. But we didn't know better at the time.

If your equipment is redundant, then you've introduced too many moving parts to your simple ecosystem. You know the old rule: Too many parts equals that many more breakdowns. Adam wasn't so much a grower or master gardener as he was a handyman. Much of his time and energy was spent running around trying to fix broken equipment. At that point, you're just killing plants because your system is getting in the way of the product's growth cycle.

To be fair to both of us, the looming disaster wasn't all our fault. As our second harvest was coming close to fruition, our roof sprang a leak. The landlord summoned a roofer who swooped in to patch the leak with tar and pebble. But the blowtorch he used to seal the tar set fire to the roof's insulation.

Smoke started pouring into our workspace.

Other than the roofer, no one was on site at the time. Even though they managed to suppress the fire, the smoke damage was extensive.

Plants breathe through their leaves. Too many of ours got a lung-ful of smoke. They were goners in a matter of days. Our second harvest was as disappointing as the first.

I had private talks with Mr. Pink where I'd express my frustrations, and he was always a good listener, a true mensch to deal with. He'd let me go off on tangents, and then he'd bring me down to earth. "Okay," he'd say, "you've been fucking this up, so how are we going to turn it around? Here's what I'd do . . ."

I have always appreciated his advice.

I took Adam aside one day and tried to make sure he understood how serious our predicament was. "We have to hit our numbers next time," I said, "or we can't pay our rent. Do you get that? We're not fucking around anymore. It has to come in high."

I didn't think it was unreasonable to shoot for seven pounds of product. Seven pounds would put us at $28,000, enough to put us ahead for three months. And the harvest after that would be gravy. We just needed to turn it around—fast.

"It's not fair that you're putting all this pressure on me," Adam said. "You should have known. You can't expect this of me. I told you when we started that it would take time to dial this in, man."

"No," I said. "No, you didn't say it takes time to dial in. You said we would be up and running, no problem."

I could sense that we had a fundamental problem, but I was not able to nail down exactly what it was. But one day, when I ran into Adam building light hangers out of PVC pipe and rope, I asked why he didn't just go to the grow store downtown and buy some professional-grade brackets to hang our lights.

"Can't do it," he said, shaking his head. "When they see you come in to buy all that stuff for lights, they *know* you're growing weed. They copy down your license plate number and give it to the cops."

Oh shit, I thought. I can't believe what I'm hearing.

I'm sure he believed every word of what he was saying, but all I heard was the old marijuana paranoia. The same sort of fears that

I'd heard from the naysayers among my family and friends ever since I'd embarked on this adventure. People still couldn't get it into their heads that marijuana was legal now. We had a license. We were legit. There was no longer any reason to fear walking into a gardening center and buying tons of lights. *That's what you do when you grow legal marijuana.*

But there, in a nutshell, I had seen Adam's biggest problem.

At heart he was a basement grower who loved marijuana. He knew exactly how to grow six to ten plants. He had no clue how to grow two thousand.

He may have spent fifteen years growing weed, but he'd been running scared the whole time. He'd done it under the cover of darkness, policing his every move so that whatever behavior he revealed to the outside world did not betray his secret. Never in a million years would he install a state-of-the-art light system by hiring an electrician. No, he'd do it himself, just to stay under the radar. He was a DIY guy at heart. It was all he knew, and he had trouble thinking big.

Once I understood where he was coming from, I saw it everywhere. It was etched into every piece of equipment in our supply chain.

In the world of business, legal business, you didn't always start out big, but you started out *boldly.* You had to. You needed big profits as soon as possible, or your venture was doomed.

In the world of the illegal grower, staying small was how you survived. You grew enough for yourself, your friends . . . and that's it. Maybe if you were really bold, you grew a little to sell. But when that happened, it was scary. Growing was bad enough; that one prospective grower I'd interviewed had gotten eight years in prison for that felony alone. Growing and selling was enough to bring The Man down on your head with a vengeance.

Wow. Here I was, planning to take the medical marijuana market in Denver by storm and the whole time it was as if I were driving into my future in a gas-guzzling car with an eight-track tape on the stereo.

So I suppose I shouldn't have been surprised the day Adam called me to give me the news on our third harvest. I was driving in the car with my wife.

"Yes?" I said expectantly.

"Four pounds," I heard him say.

"Shit," I said. "You know what that means, right? We talked about this. We're finished. We can't pay our rent next month."

He started to say he was sorry, but I heard it all as an excuse. I hung up the phone and sulked.

"What happened?" my wife said.

I didn't want to tell her. I felt uncomfortable. After all, she'd been so ashamed of my new venture that she'd refused to tell her father about it.

"It's nothing," I said, shrugging my shoulders. "It's just . . . our numbers are down for the third harvest."

My mind was racing. What was I going to tell Mr. Pink? We had used up our seed money in nine months' time. Now we were officially out of cash. I tried to calm myself, but it was tough. What I was thinking, but did not say, was *We are fucked, we are fucked, we are fucked.*

"I told you so," my wife said.

I clenched my jaw, tensed the muscles across my back and shoulders, and ratcheted my blood pressure way up. My mind raced. My field of vision narrowed as I squeezed the steering wheel. We may have been driving in silence, but I was screaming in my mind the whole time.

4

THE BEAUTY
OF FAILURE

SO OUR INITIAL ENTRY INTO THE LEGAL MARIJUANA IN-
dustry was a financial failure.

The only reasonable response to that situation was to try again.

Contrary to what people think, having failures—yes, multiple
failures—does not necessarily mean that your business will fail. All it
means is that the course of action you took did not bear fruit *that time
around*. It's possible that that course of action will *never* bear fruit. It's
equally possible that that course of action *could* bear fruit sometime
in the future, *given a set of subtly different circumstances*.

I see this a lot among entrepreneurs. They all profess to accept
that business, like life, is about trial and error, but then they take very
few chances. Face it: Failure is etched into every strand of our DNA.
It's our human legacy. A baby takes her first few steps and falls. Does
she sit there and resolve never to walk again? No—she gets right up
and tries again. She's determined to claim her birthright as a bipedal
organism.

If you are too risk averse, you will never learn anything. Failures
are instructive. They force us to grow. If you could teach all there
was to know about business in a business school, every new start-up

would succeed. But that's impossible. Failures are the critical 90 per-cent—the stuff they can't teach in school.

I can say this now, with the aid of hindsight, as the founder of a business that makes millions a year growing and selling legal mari-juana. But I assure you that I was not spouting such wisdom back in 2010, after my first attempts in the cannabis industry imploded.

No. Back then I was pissed—but resolved to do better and ready to fight on.

I knew we had to try again. I had to sit down with Mr. Pink and investigate our options.

I had been around the block enough times to know that I was merely looking at Failure No. 1. There would be more. (You'll hear about them, believe me.) People who were around me during this time sometimes found the courage to ask: How do you know you can make this work? Didn't you recently preside over the failure of your own real estate company? You didn't try to revive *that* failing business. Why redouble your efforts on behalf of this strange new business of weed?

My answer is simple. At that point in time, there's a critical ele-ment that weed had that no other industry had: opportunity.

In 2010, the world economy was in near collapse. Existing indus-tries, from real estate to banking to technology to consumer goods, were all being challenged by the largest market downturn in recent memory.

Weed was wide open.

Just because we had enjoyed our first spectacular failure did not mean weed had gone bust. Far from it. The profits were out there. We just had to get more creative and put into practice the painful knowledge that we had just paid six figures to acquire.

I had put the word out that I was looking for a new grower. Every time I met a new one, I was more than aware that I was no longer approaching our conversation as a neophyte. I was asking bet-ter questions.

Can you show a sample of your product?

What kind of system do you use for your grow?

What brands of equipment do you like, and why?

What kind of system would you recommend for me, a guy who's licensed to grow nearly two thousand plants?

What's your ideal system going to cost me?

How long will it take you to get the system optimized and operating at 100 percent?

The last question was obviously critical. Our business was running on fumes, and not the kind our customers enjoyed inhaling. Mr. Pink and I had had our heart-to-heart talk, and it wasn't looking good. He had a lot riding on this business, well beyond the money he'd sunk into it. He was a lifelong Coloradan and was personal friends with our two landlords. If we couldn't pay our rent, it would be a colossal embarrassment for him.

Yet he didn't once flinch from the awful task ahead of him. He sucked it up. He phoned each of those friends in turn and asked to sit and talk about our problem. One option, clearly, was to liquidate our meager assets and turn over whatever we earned to our landlords. But that option meant we were walking away from the cannabis industry for good. The other option was convincing them to stick with us until we hit upon a better harvest and made good on our lease.

"How can we get the numbers up?" Mr. Pink asked.

I'd been talking with a couple of promising growers, Brandon and Kim, whom I'd met through the dispensaries I sold to. Some of those dispensaries also bought regularly from Brandon and Kim. They were not a couple, by the way, just two individuals who had independently earned a reputation for good work. What I'd seen of their product was top-notch, but to get it, we needed reliable, state-of-the-art equipment that was light-years more sophisticated than the jerry-rigged budget system Adam and I had cobbled together.

Raising marijuana was now looking like an expensive, complex enterprise. But if you set aside a lot of the bullshit and looked at the problem as simply as possible, it boiled down to an equation anyone could understand:

More lights = More pounds

More pounds = More money

I could buy more lights piecemeal, the way Adam and I were doing, or we could hire some contractors to install lighting and an air handling system, but that would require an efficient design. We'd need the services of a commercial architect, and we'd need to pull numerous permits from the city.

"How much are we talking?" Mr. Pink asked.

"Half a million to do it right."

Mr. Pink could have said no. He could have thrown me out of his house. He could have told me he had already talked to our landlords, we're liquidating everything, we are getting out from under this debacle so I can save some face with my friends.

Instead, he said, "If you can get that much money elsewhere, I'm still in."

I'd been talking to contractors to get a feel for the cost of the renovations. One of them happened to mention some friends out in Los Angeles—a retired athlete and a one-time actor—who were interested in investing in some businesses, particularly in the hot new cannabis market.

The longer I am in this business, the more I realize that you can never predict who is going to turn out to be a diehard marijuana fan. I have met highly successful attorneys and physicians who treat their chronic pain or daily stress by smoking marijuana. I once met an elderly woman—an insanely wealthy individual from a highborn family—who confided in me that she smoked marijuana every day. Many actors and athletes prefer marijuana over alcohol, possibly because alcohol can mean hangovers and extra calories, but they are ever aware of a damning double standard that forces them to hide their marijuana use. An athlete who drinks to blow off steam on his time off, for example, is unlikely to garner bad press or be penalized by his team or his sponsors. A marijuana user will. Athletes have been suspended from the team and lost their endorsement contracts over infractions of this kind, so they take pains to hide their use of marijuana.

"You should talk to them," the contractor said. "Make it happen. Don't sit on this. They're serious."

I made a note of it. "Seriously? I'll call them right away."

Then I got busy with the architect. Got mired in wastewater issues down at city hall.

After a handful of phone conversations, and before ever seeing our facility, our new friends from LA cut us checks. As we'd anticipated, both wanted to remain silent partners. They were more interested in raking in a decent return than participating in our business in any way. All told, thanks to them, our bank account had risen by the amount of $495,000.

Every dollar had to count. I couldn't fuck around anymore. I was playing with other people's money now, and they would be carefully watching what I did with it.

One day, I pulled Adam aside and gave him the bad news. He must have seen it coming and took it like a man.

He was out.

Brandon and Kim were in.

I had created another opportunity to get it right. The clouds lifted, and I had hope again.

I decided on a two-prong approach: We'd hire a contractor to get started on the renovations, hard-wiring us for a ninety-two-light facility, while Brandon and Kim would establish a temporary, twenty-five-light grow in the building next door. Yes, it meant more money. A second lease. A second rent payment every month. More permits. More headaches. But we could not afford to wait while our first building was renovated. We were too desperate to establish a revenue stream.

We weren't the only ones. You have to recall that everything we were doing was playing out against the backdrop of the worst financial crisis in the United States since the Great Depression. I'd lost my last company due to the housing crisis, and millions of other Americans were struggling with the ripples emanating from that downturn. Our contractor, who I'll call Sam, was the same guy who'd put us in touch with our new investors. He was the patriarch of a construction firm with a long history in Denver. I thought I'd made a solid decision when I'd hired them to be our general contractor. Mr. Pink and I both knew him, and our kids all went to school together. What could be more stable than a firm that's been in business more than ninety-three years in the same city?

Well, I was wrong.

The work on our grow moved glacially. I'd go down there some days to find no one on the premises. Other days, a guy I called Bob the Builder was the only one working in that 5,000-square-foot space. Some days, I'd call and text Sam incessantly to light a fire under his ass.

What the hell is the holdup, man?

Remember what I was telling you about failure? Failure is so endemic to the human species that even if you're not the one failing, you can pretty much count on those around you failing. It's virtually impossible to guard against such a happenstance. Most times you just can't see it coming.

Contractors do a lot of their business on credit. They buy tons of supplies in expectation that their clients will cut them a check in the next week, the next month, the next year. If a customer's slow or the customer goes belly-up, the contractor's got no choice but to default on everything *he* owes. To compound the problem, in the wake of the housing crisis, a lot of tradespeople—carpenters, electricians, plumbers, and the like—were pulling up stakes, moving out of the city, or else transitioning to new jobs. Sam was short on men, short on cash, short on supplies, short on answers.

Months passed.

I knew something was wrong. It was obvious. I called Mr. Pink when I finally got the news I knew was coming. Our contractor was going out of business, another terrible casualty of a tanking worldwide market. Sam was supremely sorry, but he just couldn't make good on the job. Yes, he'd taken a lot of our money—our *investors'* money—but he couldn't pay it back. He'd spent it all trying to keep another job afloat, and that would come back to bite him in the ass later. That would be his cross to bear in court one day.

It was looking ugly.

Picture Mr. Pink and me sitting in his study, holding our heads.

Picture Mr. Pink grilling me on what we were going to say *this time around* to our landlords, not to mention our investors and creditors.

Holy shit, we thought, we're about to lose it *again*.

There was just one shining light in all this. Brandon and Kim had worked wonders with the grow next door. Brandon possessed the greenest of thumbs, and he had a knack for sourcing some fantastic strains, like SkunkBerry which was a cross between two standard marijuana strains, purple skunk and blueberry. But they came together beautifully and would one day help us win acclaim for our company. Another great strain Brandon mastered growing for us was the famous sativa, Jack Herer, named after the late but well-regarded cannabis activist. When you take a puff of Jack Herer, you feel like you've just downed a couple of Red Bulls and you're ready to stay up all night talking with friends you haven't seen in years. For me personally, it's like one too many cups of coffee, but it's a fine strain nonetheless.

Our harvests, even with the twenty-five lights we had, were increasing. One rule of thumb in the cannabis business is that each light will generate about 1 pound of product every other month. Or, to put it another way, ten lights would yield 5 pounds a month. Only, in Brandon and Kim's hands, each light was yielding about 1.3

pounds every other month—a substantial bunch of buds! Suddenly we had about $40,000 a month coming in the door. Understand: This was not our profit, just the revenue stream. But those harvests helped us stay afloat and lessened the sting of our diminishing bank account.

Some days I'd go down to the grow and stand there, drinking in the nearly tropical moisture and the glistening leaves and the sweet smell of those buds, and I'd feel my blood pressure drop. There is something transcendent about simply being in the presence of plants with which you are so inextricably bound. After so many years of being detached from the meaning of working with Nature, this experience had become magical for me. I was awake, alive, and thriving when I was around the plants. I imagined I could feel them growing. Hell, when I was around them, I felt I was growing, too.

I love you and support you, I'd tell those plants. If you guys keep living and producing, we will make it.

The plants stared back at me wordlessly, not acknowledging a thing about my dilemma. But they kept growing.

A thought occurred to me: Some months ago, we'd made a sizable payment to Sam's electrical subcontractor. Sam was going out of business, but the electrician probably wasn't.

More lights equals more pounds.

More pounds equals more money.

I got on the horn with the electrician. Could he see his way clear to finishing the job?

He pulled the paperwork and did the math. Yeah, he admitted, we still had a credit with the company. But he was wary about walking onto Sam's unfinished job. He was concerned that we'd blame him for everything. "If you promise not to sue us, we'll come down and finish the job."

"I'm not suing you," I said. "Get down here. I have to get this system upgraded. I need more power and I need to get those lights up and running."

To make him feel completely comfortable, I signed a document to this effect, and the company came back to finish the job that it had originally signed on to do.

More lights, more buds, more money.

Yes, we needed to do more than just electrical work. But if I could get those lights up in the original building and start generating more income, I could act as general contractor myself and hire my own subcontractors to get the rest of the job done. I was hoping to save a little money, but unfortunately it all had to be done to code, down to the last detail. The city inspectors had insisted on that, and later I would be grateful.

The electricians came and got us on line, finishing the job quickly. Before each room of lights went live, I had Brandon and Kim start a fresh batch of clones. You'd think that with all this turmoil that the plants would be affected, but that wasn't the case at all. Remember what I said earlier about how we can't cram Nature? How we can't force it to do what it isn't programmed to do? There's something comforting in that. Something earnest and right and predictable.

We humans were scurrying around, our tempers boiling. Mr. Pink and I were worried that we'd lose our shirts for the second time. Sam was grappling with his failing business. The electricians were worried about being sued.

And the plants just kept growing.

They stuck to their punch clock, day in, day out.

So long as Brandon and Kim were there to water them, feed them, nurture and love them, the plants did the only thing they knew how to do. They were inextricably connected to the rhythm of the universe.

One day our growers called with the harvest figure, and I had to stop what I was doing and ask them to repeat it.

Then I called Mr. Pink at work.

"Are you shitting me?"

"Fifty pounds, man!"

Do the math with me, won't you? With a wholesale value of about $2,500 a pound, that harvest would earn us $125,000 from the dispensaries that were now clamoring for our goods. And since Brandon and Kim had staggered our resources, we had another harvest coming in less than a month.

That was very promising. We weren't out of trouble yet. We had debts to repay. And our expenses were high. Besides the cost of growing the weed, we had our rents, our seven new employees (Brandon, Kim, a grow helper, and four staffers who helped us harvest and trim), and the parade of new subcontractors. Additionally, the state had become increasingly creative about hitting the cannabis industry with a fresh menu of fees. On my desk I had a stack of about $56,000 in fees to pay to various taxing and licensing entities in Colorado.

But it didn't matter. We had had our *failures,* but we had not *failed.* The plants were growing. We were bringing in the buds. The axiom *More lights, more money* had held true.

The cash was rolling in—finally.

We just had nowhere to put it.

5

DON'T BANK ON IT

WHEN OUR BUSINESS WAS FINALLY UP AND RUNNING AT a nice clip, I'd occasionally meet people who wanted to tell me about their personal relationship with this joyous little plant. Mostly people liked to tell me how much they loved weed and how happy they were that it was finally legal, at least medically, in their home state.

At a party one night, I met a man I'll call Joe. He was in his early thirties. A handsome guy who happened to have been born near Chihuahua, Mexico.

His story was very different from that of the marijuana lovers. His was a story of survival, grit, determination—and money. Money to pay rent, for food, and to care for his family.

When he was still in his teens, Joe helped his family survive by selling marijuana. He'd start by scraping together $10, which he'd use to buy a 2-kilo, plastic-wrapped "brick" of marijuana from the local honchos in his community. He'd stick the brick in his back-pack, kiss his mother and sisters good-bye, and set out for southern Colorado in the United States of America.

On foot.

That's right—he walked across the Mexico–U.S. border, dodging the U.S. Border Patrol, then walked through Arizona and New Mexico, way up into Colorado. His destination was Pueblo, Colorado, where he had some friends and contacts. There, after a number of days walking, he sold his precious cargo for more than $3,000 a pound. When the job was done and he'd rested up, he'd buy a ticket back south on a bus, his backpack stuffed with about $15,000 in cash.

Once home, he and his family used that money to support themselves, until it was time to hit the road again. Joe made this dangerous odyssey several times through his teens. He was never caught.

I was blown away by his story.

Perhaps you are offended by the notion of foreign citizens exploiting gaps in the U.S. legal system to carry out illicit transactions like this. Okay. I get it. But I'd like you to try to muster some compassion for a young man who would make such an arduous trek, on foot, to help his family. When I heard his story, there were no pearl-handled semiautomatic pistols, no drug lord's overdecorated lair, anywhere in the tale. I heard nothing but a tale of survival. Imagine being asked to hunt an animal whose meat would keep your family alive but that might kill you in the hunting. This was the risk Joe had taken as a kid. When I was riding bikes or playing football in my neighborhood, Joe was walking nearly a thousand miles and risking his life. Think what kind of life he and his family must have had, that he would be forced into such labor to satisfy our very American needs. Is Joe the cause or the result of our illegal marijuana market?

If you can be compassionate about Joe, then I think you would agree that he was in as much danger *going* to his destination in the United States as he was *returning* home to Mexico. Numbers are sketchy on this score, but the rate at which Mexicans are losing their lives to the drug trade is obscenely high. By one estimate, fifty thousand Mexicans died violently in just six years, between 2006 and 2012.

In both situations, Joe was carrying something of value. Marijuana on the way north and tons of cash on the way home.

I'll bet most of you reading this have never carried that much money on your person, even if you had access to it. It just isn't safe. There was a time, probably as recently as the early twentieth century, when people *did* keep their money and precious valuables tucked under their mattresses, but those days are gone for the majority of people who live in nations with stable banking systems. I know people like to bitch about customer service and interest rates and hidden fees, but whether they've thought of it or not, such banking systems have imbued their lives with a good deal of security and stability. In the United States, once money is deposited in a bank, it's insured by the federal government, and citizens can get on with their lives—pay bills, transfer funds, withdraw cash for gifts—on a whim, without ever worrying if their nest egg is safe and sound. Yes, FDIC insurance is not unlimited—only $250,000 per depositor is covered—but at least it's there.

But as I'm writing this, the people who work in the new legal marijuana economy do not enjoy that same privilege. They're as vulnerable as that nervous teenager on the bus heading south to his family. At any moment, their earnings can be ripped off. At any moment, the hard work they've pumped into their business can disappear forever—all because their country won't give them a simple privilege the rest of us enjoy.

A bank account.

THE BANK MANAGER'S EXPRESSION was one you never want to see: part angst, part embarrassment, part distaste. Like it was our fault that he was this uncomfortable in his job.

We'd been banking at this particular institution for eighteen months, ever since the day Mr. Pink had opened an account for our company and wired in our first big infusion of seed money.

From the beginning, we had been completely transparent about our business plans. My attorney had urged me to be "open and notorious." From day one I had followed a piece of similar advice proffered by my accountant: "If you're serious about getting into the legal marijuana business, don't hide a damned thing. Make it completely clear to everyone you meet that this is what you do. You don't ever want anyone to come back later and say you lied to them."

Our banker knew what we did for living. That was what made this conversation so awful for him. He'd been fine with our business for more than a year. Now he was not so fine anymore.

"You guys are great clients," he said. "But we can no longer service your account."

"Service?"

"We cannot continue to have your account here at this bank."

"This branch, or the whole bank?"

"The whole bank."

"Oh," I said, "You're kicking us out."

"No," he said. "That's not strictly true. My advice is to use the money that's in the account right now. But you will not be able to make any more deposits. When the money's used up, we'll close the account." The bank also sent us a nice letter spelling out these terms and stating our undesirability as clients. I saved it as a souvenir.

Why was this happening? Because, according to federal banking law, we were drug dealers, of course.

See, back when Mr. Pink opened the account, the bank managers had assumed that if a depositor was legal and licensed by the state of Colorado, that depositor was welcome as a customer. After all, no one wants to do business with illegal drug dealers, right? *Legal* drug dealers were on the up-and-up.

But as word trickled from the Colorado bank to its board of directors and risk mitigation committees, the powers that be had carefully considered the corporation's position and nixed the idea of legal marijuana business checking accounts.

The reason made sense; it just didn't bode well for anyone we knew in the cannabis industry. Regardless of whether a bank is head-quartered in a weed-friendly state or not, it is a federal institution. In order to be part of the Federal Deposit Insurance Corporation program that insures all accounts, U.S. banks must play ball with the federal government. And growing and selling marijuana is still a federal crime. Our bank reasoned that it would lose its charter or be criminally prosecuted if the federal government learned that it was doing business with drug dealers. So our bank had made the decision to show us the door.

We could live with the decision, and we did exactly as the manager suggested. When we spent our last dime, we closed the account and opened another at a local bank. We were completely up front about our business, and the new bank didn't give us any trouble—then.

That relationship lasted a year before the second bank kicked us out.

The same angst, the same awkwardness, the same uncomfortable banker look, the same damn form letter. I kept that one, too.

Around the same time, another local bank in Denver announced that it was offering commercial marijuana checking accounts. To bank there, all you needed to do was show that you were a state-licensed marijuana dealer.

Great, we thought. It's about time someone figured out a way to make this work. We rushed over and opened our third account. We were not the only ones. It seemed as if every grower or dispensary owner in the city had gravitated here. We were all so grateful to have finally found a home. But we should have seen it coming. Sooner or later, someone at headquarters connected the dots and realized that the bank was leaving itself open to federal prosecution. When that happened, we were out on the street again. We got another letter, and yes, I kept that one, too. I was thinking that if this kept up, I might be able to wallpaper a restroom in one of our dispensaries someday.

It seemed only fitting, I thought, as I slipped the letter in with the others.

We didn't give up. I mean, we assumed—as any businessperson would—that the law was on our side. Sooner or later, we would prevail. *Our businesses were licensed by the state! We paid taxes! How could we be denied access to the banking system?* It was absurd.

But that absurdity was boundless. We kept moving on, thinking that eventually we would hit upon a bank that had sorted out this issue internally and would welcome our business. But that was not to be. At one point, we were kicked out of three banks in five weeks.

By then, it was quite clear that every legal cannabis company in the state and the nation was in the same position.

Early in 2014, the White House announced that it supported changing federal bank guidelines to allow licensed cannabis providers access to banks. I and my fellow entrepreneurs were hopeful for about fifteen minutes, until we realized that it would take an act of Congress to get the banks to change. At this writing, we are still locked out.

What does that mean for us?

Well, if you'd like to see what our lives are like sometime, all you have to do is try to pay your monthly bills totally in cash. This was no doubt possible in simpler times, but it's virtually impossible today. Yes, you can probably drive to an office locally to pay your cable TV, gas, or electric bills in cash. And some people may be able to pay their rent or mortgages in person, but most of us need to transmit those funds online or at least through the postal service. You could buy money orders each time, but that will quickly become tedious. So much of your time will be spent in long lines at the post office that you will start to wonder if you're wasting your time. (Hint: You are.)

Now imagine having to pay *huge* bills in cash—amounts in the tens of thousands. Welcome to my world.

It's not easy running a million-dollar company in an all-cash position, but it can be done. For one thing, our firm stopped sharing our information with banks. They're not your friends these days, anyway. First thing we did was form a holding company, through which we can flow enough cash to write checks to pay taxes and the other bills that truly require having a bank account.

When it comes time to pay our state taxes, we literally walk cash into the Colorado Department of Revenue office, which is next door to the gold-domed Colorado State Capitol Building, and hand over the Benjamins with our tax forms. Our federal taxes must be remitted electronically—no cash or checks accepted. Paying those requires the same kind of ingenuity we use to pay any large bill from a vendor or contractor.

In the eyes of the federal government, we are laundering money every time we do this. But as yet no law enforcement agency has cracked down on us. In his 2014 announcement, President Obama instructed the Justice Department to leave cannabis entrepreneurs alone if they were "in clear and unambiguous compliance with state marijuana law." But that instruction was not terribly clear, either, and certainly did not carry the full weight of law behind it.

It's almost as if we're trapped in bureaucratic limbo: Until Congress sprouts the balls to deal with the issue, everyone on the federal level is content to look the other way. Meaningful legislation will come inevitably, but that will mean breaking it to the American people that Congress is finally saying okay to marijuana. Our representatives in DC know that once they open a door, they won't be able to close it. If it's okay to deposit legal marijuana money in federal banks, then why is marijuana still illegal on the federal level?

You see? It's a slippery slope.

So: Where does that leave us? Well, for all other transactions, we use cash. The more the better, because the more cash we can offload, the more we can invest in expansion, say, or use in some other substantive ways, the less we have to hold and hide.

If it sounds ridiculous, insane, and dangerous to do business this way—I agree. When you consider that every person in the legal marijuana business in Colorado must wear a badge clipped to their shirt at all times and that they are not permitted to carry a weapon to protect themselves, it's even more ludicrous. What could be more dangerous than proclaiming to the world through a badge you must wear that you are unarmed and that you are most likely carrying weed or copious quantities of cash?

Many of the cannabis firms I know have signed with security firms—bodyguards and armored truck providers—to safely convey their cash from their places of business to the various safes hidden throughout the city. We follow strict protocols to pick up cash from our stores. We installed cameras and alarms and pricey security systems. But those services and equipment don't come cheap, and there are always days when you need to ferry a few thousand dollars to a vendor by yourself.

We don't like doing it. In fact, we hate it. But we do it anyway, usually looking over our shoulders. Most of the people we deal with—like the architect I mentioned at the beginning of this book—now know that they wouldn't get our business if they weren't comfortable accepting at least a little cash.

Please don't misunderstand: I am grateful for the abundance in my life and business, but cash leaves me feeling vulnerable. Yes, Denver is a relatively safe city. In all the time I've worked in the industry, I know of no one who was ripped off while transporting money earned in the legal marijuana industry.

The danger of being robbed aside, there's another reason legitimate businesses don't traffic in cash: It's a pain in the ass.

Think about it: At most businesses of our size, the chief executive and shareholders don't meet to discuss paying bills. All that stuff is managed by the company's accountants. You authorize a check, the checks get cut, and someone in middle management signs them before they're shipped out. Case closed. You don't call a board meeting to figure out a plan to pay your electrician, no matter how much he's charging you. Doing so is an amateurish way to run a company.

SO MANY OF OUR POP CULTURE REFERENCES associate copious quantities of cash with illegal activities. Who can forget those scenes in Brian De Palma's *Scarface* where Tony Montana's crew pulls up in front of a bank and whisks duffel bags of illegal drug money inside to be laundered? At first, the corrupt bank manager is happy to have their business, but as time goes on, he's increasingly unnerved by the ceaseless stream.

The chemistry teacher–turned–meth kingpin Walter White in the *Breaking Bad* cable TV series goes through a similar process of cash fatigue. First, he gets by laundering cash through his lawyer's office. Then he buys a legitimate business—a car wash—to be able to launder it all. His wife, Skyler, becomes increasingly frustrated with him, because no matter how creatively she cooks the books, it's not enough to hide the flow of cash. By the end of the series, Walter's world unravels and he is reduced to desperately burying millions in the desert.

These stories are meant to be entertainment with a little bit of morality tossed in for good measure. The cash Montana and White earn become symbols for their criminal obsessions gone wrong, gone awry, gone out of whack. Their stories are actually not far from the truth. In 2011, Mexican authorities raided a Tijuana home of an illegal drug kingpin and found more than $15 million in cash. That's a lot of green, but it pales in comparison to the largest drug cash seizure in history: $206 million, which was lying around the home of an influential player in Mexico's meth industry.

The legal cannabis movement is all about making things right again. This plant was maligned by the federal government for nearly a hundred years. Now the cash raised by legal marijuana enterprises is supporting the budgets of at least twenty U.S. states, with more on the way. It's paying for schools, it's helping our neediest citizens, and it's helping to balance state budgets at a time in the nation's history when states need it most.

The U.S. Treasury, via the Internal Revenue Service, happily sticks our money in its hip pocket but refuses to give us the one thing we need to be recognized as capitalists and full-fledged partners in American productivity.

I am not Tony Montana.

I am not Walter White.

Yet every day I commit two federal crimes. I grow and sell marijuana, and I "launder" the money I earn from those crimes by passing that cash on to my employees, contractors, and landlords. Being the nice, law-abiding drug dealer that I am, I also pay my state and federal taxes with the money I earn from those enterprises. It's downright Orwellian.

We are not criminals, but the law is forcing us to behave like them.

6

THE HAZE OF
PARANOIA

I HAD JUST PARKED IN THE LOT OF A DENVER SAFEWAY. When the other car drove up, I waved hi and popped my trunk.

Money changed hands.

I slipped the cash in my pocket and helped my new friend stash the product in the trunk of his car. The product consisted of fifty or so tiny sprouts peeking out of containers of damp soil.

Just as we were about to go our separate ways, we heard the *woop, woop, woop* of a police cruiser's siren as the vehicle pulled into the lot beside us.

A woman police officer got out, her hands lightly grazing the grip of her holstered pistol.

"Is something wrong, Officer?"

"I got a call that people were trading . . . *plants* in the parking lot," she said. "Do you mind telling me what you're doing?"

It was early autumn 2009 and I had been in the business just a few months. I had done everything by the book. I had followed all the state regs, even ones that the state's marijuana regulators were still hazy on. Our industry was so new, so five minutes old, that the authorities were interpreting the law on the fly.

This was not the first police encounter I'd ever had in my life, but it was the first since I'd started growing marijuana.

"Do you mind telling me what's going on here?" she said again.

"Not at all, ma'am," I said. "This gentleman and I are both in the legal marijuana business. I just sold him my extra plants. You'll find fifty clones in the trunk of his car, and the money's in my pocket."

"Okay . . ." she said, her voice trailing. The look in her eyes was already anxious and judgmental. I had said the magic word. The word that set many people in law enforcement on edge: *marijuana*.

"Give me your identification, and you wait right here."

At the time, Colorado had not yet rolled out its medical marijuana dealer badges. We used our red cards as part of our state documentation. So I passed her my red card and driver's license, and so did my new friend. And she retreated to her police cruiser.

I was sweating bullets. I had never been in a situation like this. You'll recall that the state of Colorado had a rule that said that for every medical patient I enrolled, I could grow six plants. That meant that our grow facility always had the maximum number of plants we could legally have at any one time. The minute our clones—small plants that had been clipped from a mother plant and rooted in soil—took us over the legal limit, we were obliged to destroy them or sell them to someone else who could legally use them. That's all I was doing. I just didn't anticipate that someone would call the cops on us.

My mind was racing.

I was terrified. I forced myself to think logically, rationally. What should I do? If she arrested me right now, they would probably impound my vehicle. If so, any valuables on my person would probably be checked into the police station.

Planning for what then felt inevitable, I started removing my watch, my wallet, my wedding band, anything I thought was too valuable to be hanging around a police station evidence locker.

As I finished stashing this stuff in my glove compartment, the police officer stepped out of her vehicle and was waiting to resume our conversation.

As I stepped over to her, her hand came up, my documentation held lightly between her index and middle fingers.

"Here you go," she said.

And then she stopped, my ID dangling from her fingers.

"You know you're playing with fire, don't you?" she said.

"Excuse me?"

And off she went, launching into an angry, two-minute lecture.

We were ruining ourselves.

We were ruining the city.

We were ruining children.

How could she protect us?

We had to be careful.

People killed over this stuff.

Marijuana was wrong. It would always be wrong.

But then, as she was talking, there was this moment when I could sense that she was running out of steam. The fire in her eyes was dying, just as it became clear that we were off the hook.

She wasn't going to bust us.

She knew that we weren't the same as the criminals and drug dealers she and her fellow cops saw every day.

We were licensed; the law was on our side.

The law was on our side!

The police officer's rant was really more about *her* frustrations. The newfound complexities of her job. The world she knew was changing, and from this day forward, she would have to delineate in her mind between *legal* marijuana dealers and *illegal* marijuana dealers.

"I know it's legal," she said, "but no one's telling us how to handle this stuff."

If people could now buy and sell marijuana like geraniums in the parking lot of a Safeway, what was her role? Was she supposed to stand by and watch? Check it out? Ignore her dispatcher's call? Laugh it off? What?

Her supervisors hadn't briefed her on any of this stuff, which only made her feel . . . edgy, uncomfortable, and isolated.

She handed back my documents. "You're free to go."

MARIJUANA IS MOST CLOSELY ASSOCIATED with feelings of euphoria. But if you don't watch what you're doing, you can have dysphoric effects from the drug, too. One of the most common is a sense of paranoia—a feeling that you're about to be busted when the reality is just the opposite.

From my earliest days in the business, I noticed that a bizarre paranoia surrounded the industry. The funny thing about it was that it was coming from people who *weren't* smoking marijuana.

I call this paranoia marijuana legalization denial syndrome. Citizens in the grip of MLDS are incapable of accepting marijuana's legality on its face. There has to be a catch, they think.

You'll recall that when Mr. Pink and I first invested in the legal cannabis business, our spouses worried that the law might be repealed and everyone who had gone into the legal marijuana business would be instantly arrested without a chance to defend themselves. Longtime marijuana smokers fretted that the law was a ploy to root them out and get them on the record so they could be arrested later, when the law was repealed. Certainly it wouldn't be the first time the government had lied to its citizens.

Mr. Pink and I didn't make a big deal of this, but we, too, worried about it privately. For that reason, many of my leases were negotiated to expire on inauguration day, every fourth year, on the twenty-first of January—just in case the new presidential and gubernatorial administrations and state legislature were unfavorable to our business. We hypothesized that the previous autumn's election would give us some hint if they intended to shut us down. If anti-marijuana candidates won the election, we would know by November. That would give us until January to conclude operations and then not renew our lease. This was the closest we ever came to an emergency exit plan, and one we needed uniquely for this type of business. It's also one we've never needed to employ, thankfully.

When we started going downtown to apply for a host of paperwork—from business licenses to building permits—we were met with quiet resistance ripped from the MLDS playbook. Some city and state employees were solidly in the grip of MLDS. "I know it's the law," was their attitude, "but I haven't been told how to handle it and I am not going out of my way for people like you." This was the first time in my life that I felt the sting of a negative stereotype. These employees assumed that I was a criminal who was trying to exploit a loophole in the law. Let me say for the record that there is no such loophole; the law was as unambiguous as possible. Marijuana was legal. But now I was being confronted with a form of prejudice. It wasn't a typical example of prejudice, but it was prejudice just the same. It could only be met by my own quiet persistence and compassion.

"I'm opening a medical marijuana business," I'd say. "I have the legal paperwork to prove it. We just need a business license."

"There's no such thing as a business license for medical marijuana."

Or . . .

"I need a building permit for a medical marijuana growing facility," I'd say.

"Can't help you," the bureaucrat at the desk would say. "There's no such thing as building code for a marijuana grow."

Well, duh. The law was so new, no one really knew what sort of specs such a building should have. But were they really going to sit there and tell me they couldn't help me?

Turns out, they were.

Nothing irritates an entrepreneur as much as a pencil pusher who can't be motivated to solve problems and think his or her way out of a situation.

Surely they had heard that marijuana was legal in the state?

Yep. They just hadn't been told what to do about it. And they couldn't be bothered to look into it. They had a break coming up in a few minutes.

I was less irritated when I visited the state offices that were charged with regulating our new industry and enforcing the laws surrounding it. There, the folks wanted to be helpful but were underfunded and overwhelmed.

Over at the Department of Health, the office in charge of processing all those medical marijuana red cards was hopelessly backlogged. All over the state, prescribing physicians were giving their patients a temporary card with the promise that their official red card would arrive from the state within thirty days. That office had been slammed with more than fifty thousand red card applications and had only one person to deal with it all.

The new Medical Marijuana Enforcement Division (MMED), run as part of the Colorado Department of Revenue, hadn't set up its new offices yet. It had yet to lease space, furnish the offices, and hire and train personnel. The division drew enforcement personnel from the ranks of the state police, who wore badges and carried weapons on their hips.

When the MMED first opened, it rented space in a dog track that was about to be torn down. It used to be the home of live greyhound racing. That business had stopped operating some years ago. The dirt track and manicured infield had gone to seed. On the site, an off-track betting parlor, or OTB, continued to operate. It lured a strange assortment of weathered men who all seemed to smell of stale beer and cigarettes.

The first of my many meetings with the MMED took place at the dog track, staring out at an unkempt field of tall grass. A few years later, when I'd take meetings with senior MMED officials who remembered the old dog-track days, we couldn't help reminiscing about where it had all started and how much had happened to get us where we were today. That's where I met Lewis Koski, who started as a staff-level investigator and now, at the time of this writing, is the director of the newly renamed Marijuana Enforcement Division for the Colorado Department of Revenue.

In the end, of all the people we were dealing with, the cops would turn out to be the coolest and most level-headed. And I say that in spite of my run-in with that officer in the parking lot.

I'm a law-abiding person. I wouldn't be in this business if it wasn't legal. So I tried to understand the position of everyone I was coming in contact with—cops, judges, bureaucrats—and tried to see the situation from their point of view.

When you do that, you can't help but empathize with their plight. Imagine if you have spent your entire career hearing only one message about marijuana. Imagine if you have busted thousands of people with this drug and heard nothing but excuses and professions of innocence. Imagine if you've witnessed firsthand what violent drug users and criminals have done to our cities.

You'd be suspicious if the law suddenly said marijuana was okay.

You'd feel as if the rug had been pulled out from under you.

Maybe you'd even feel betrayed by politicians and the justice system that employed you.

I empathized with them. I knew how hard the United States had worked to stem the growth of the drug trade. I had grown to adulthood in the age of First Lady Nancy Reagan's Just Say No to Drugs campaign. I had seen police officers address classrooms following the precepts outlined by the D.A.R.E. America program, which was designed to empower kids to resist the lure of drug culture.

But I was now far more educated about the history of marijuana than I had been as a teen, a young adult, or even the young father I had been just a short time ago. Because I was willing to look beyond my country's pat pronouncements about marijuana, I believed that I actually had more information at my disposal than the authorities I was meeting.

I was now more convinced than ever that our national policy on marijuana was the product of distortions, poor judgment, and injustice.

President Nixon resigned the presidency in 1974, but his hard-line legacy on marijuana has lived on and been expanded on by subsequent administrations. It's an embarrassing, appalling record. Back in 1965, only 119,000 Americans were arrested for marijuana offenses. Today, that number averages more than 800,000 Americans annually. In all, we've arrested 22 million people since the Nixon era. Today, half of all arrests are marijuana related. Not all people end up prosecuted, of course, but sentences, when they are handed down, are disproportionately harder on minorities.

Most arrests are for mere possession, and federal, state, and local governments often portray the resulting sentences as slaps on the wrist. But even if you're not imprisoned, the penalties for marijuana use and possession are often life-changing and harsh. You're fined. You end up in court. You are forced into drug rehab programs. You're saddled with a criminal record for life. You can lose your license, your kids, your home, your job, and even your right to vote. If you step out of line, you can go to jail. In his research, the investigative journalist Eric Schlosser has found that in some U.S. states, the penalties for marijuana trafficking can be harsher than the penalties for murder.

In the civil sector, the advent of drug testing has made it harder to evade punishment for occasional use. Because traces of marijuana remain in your system far longer than alcohol—as much as a month, in the case of heavy users—it's easy to paint someone as a stoner with a random test. You could end up losing your job or losing your chance of being hired, while habitual alcoholics will come off as squeaky clean until someone notices alcohol on their breath.

If we can be cynical for a second, the point I made earlier about certain industries thriving by having hemp out of the way is true for our justice system as well. As long as marijuana stays illegal, our jails stay full. Our courts stay busy and can more easily justify their expense to voters. When law-abiding people are manipulated by alarming drug arrest statistics, law enforcement agencies get funded and stay funded. Federal drug czars get to look like they're accomplishing something. Tons of rehab centers get more bodies thrust through their front door.

When you look at it this way, it's smart to bust people for marijuana. It's the best way to get the largest number of people into the revolving door of the justice system for the smallest possible infraction.

But recently, something snapped with the public. Americans slowly became more savvy about marijuana and demanded a change. In 1996 voters went to the polls in California and Arizona, demanding the right to use marijuana for medical use. When this happened, the feds overreacted, requesting money from Congress to make sure marijuana stayed illegal. Congress spent $1.5 billion between 1998 and 2011 to teach a new generation of people that marijuana was bad.

But all the legal marijuana movement needed to turn the tide was more people with more experience under their belts.

More people to realize that this much-maligned herb had legitimate medical uses.

More people to realize that responsible use of marijuana was possible.

More people to hear out the data and understand that the herb was safer in most hands than alcohol.

Some of the people who learned this firsthand were state regulators and law enforcement personnel. They needed time to start replacing their personal experience of legal marijuana with the disinformation that had been handed down as gospel for more than forty years.

It was happening right before my eyes. The paranoia was dying.

The longer I was in the legal cannabis business, the more MLDS was disappearing like a puff of smoke in the breeze.

SUMMER 2013. The burglar alarm went off at my grow facility on South Platte River Drive. By now, I'd invested nearly $600,000 in this facility. We didn't have theft insurance; at the time, no policy existed to insure a marijuana grow, legal or otherwise. A burglary would hit us hard; we couldn't afford to lose any product or equipment. No business can. The downtime and lost revenue would be devastating.

My iPhone rang. I answered in a daze. It was 1:44 a.m. "Yes?"

"Hello, Mr. Hageseth. This is Digital Safe. We have multiple alarms triggered at the facility nicknamed Platte River Garden. Would you like us to dispatch the police?"

I became fully awake in one breath. My head was completely focused.

"Which zones are alarming?" I asked, reaching for my iPad. I woke the device and launched the app through which I can watch all our security cameras.

"Zones 2, 7, 10, and 11," came the voice.

A cold chill crossed my body. "Send the cops! Send them now. This is real!"

Zone 2 was our front door, 7 was an interior motion detector, 10 was a storage closet, and 11 was the mother lode—our vault. It held tens of thousands of dollars' worth of marijuana, all packaged and ready to go.

In less than thirty seconds, I was watching the view of our security cameras live in that facility. I was watching both the bad guys drive away and the good guys—the cops—arriving. The first cop on scene radioed dispatch, and police dispatch called me moments later.

"Hello, Mr. Hageseth, Denver Police have responded to a burglar alarm at your business address on South Platte River Drive and have found evidence of a break-in. You need to go there now."

It was a hot summer's night in Colorado. It was probably seventy-five or eighty degrees at 2 a.m. I pulled on my shorts, flip-flops, and the button-down shirt I'd been wearing the day before and ran out to my car. By then marijuana had been good to me, and I was driving the car of my dreams, a convertible Porsche 911. As I drove to the facility, I couldn't resist sneaking a peek at the security camera views appearing on my phone.

When I arrived at the grow, I was initially confused because there wasn't a single cop car in sight. But when I pulled into the parking lot, I saw five of Denver's finest standing by our front door. Two had guns drawn. The other three had their hands on their weapons, which remained in their holsters.

The first cop approached me as I pulled up. I imagined what this looked like to him: a guy in a flashy sports car with the top down, driving around in the middle of the night and dressed as if he's going somewhere . . .

"Are you the owner?" he asked.

"Yes." I sensed I was about to hear another lecture about exactly how legal marijuana is, but that lecture never came.

His eyes flashed to the badge hanging around my neck. Its green background indicated that I was an associated key—an owner who worked in the cannabis business.

I could read his eyes. He was thinking, "He's legit."

"Your front door has been broken open, and it appears you have been robbed. Because of the locked doors inside, we are awaiting a K-9 unit to come and clear the building."

Well, shit, I thought. If these guys haven't figured out that this building is filled with weed, then the police dog certainly will. My body tensed.

"Do you know this is a *legal medical* marijuana grow facility?" I asked the cop, emphasizing both *legal* and *medical* . . .

"Of course we do, Mr. Hageseth. There is a whole bunch of your SkunkBerry spilled over there. We think the bad guys dropped it trying to get away." He paused and smiled. "Smells really good."

He asked me to stand behind my car until the K-9 units finished a search of the building. They wanted to be sure the bad guys weren't in there before they had me enter.

"It looks empty," one cop said. "But I need you to stay here, sir, while we check it out."

No problem, I thought.

Guns drawn, dogs at the ready, they swept the inside of the facility.

The rest of us waited outside.

A few minutes later, they emerged empty-handed and gave us the all-clear sign.

No bad guys inside.

Long story short: Some burglars had broken in. When our alarm sounded, they bolted, but not before snatching a few armfuls of harvested weed. In their haste, they dropped buds all the way out the door. The canine unit was sniffing these buds now, trampling them to such a degree that their handlers had to lead their dogs away and pick out sticky buds from their animals' paws.

The K-9 officers apologized to me for the loss of my product.

I couldn't help thinking: Wow, the world has changed!

The cops lingered in the area. Some radioed back. Some filled out paperwork.

Everyone was treating me with the utmost deference. Sir this, sir that.

"Hey," one of them said. "A friend of mine sells medical marijuana."

"Oh, really?"

"Yeah, interesting business. I tell you what . . ."

And then he launched into the sort of chat you'd have with a friendly stranger in a bar.

TWO SCENARIOS, two years apart.

In 2009, I was the subject of angry, unwarranted scrutiny for selling clones in a supermarket parking lot. In 2013, I was just another businessman.

In 2013, the cops were there to protect me and my personal property. The lessons they had learned about marijuana over their careers had changed enough to accept the reality that there were legal dealers of this product in their midst. I was stunned. We weren't the bad guys anymore.

Legal marijuana was just another thing that crooks boosted— like TVs or jewelry or cartons of cigarettes.

The world I knew was changing.

That did not mean that I was always on board with how the cops around me perceived that new world.

On another occasion, after someone had broken into a storage shed behind one of our grows, an officer took me aside and offered me some friendly advice.

"There are a lot of really bad people out there. I see them every day. And those bad people know where you are and who you are," he said. "They won't think twice about shooting and killing you to rob you. You have to protect yourself."

He was gently advising me to get a handgun. Whether he knew that was a violation of my medical marijuana license or not is irrelevant. In his worldview, guns in the hands of the right people could help save someone's life.

"If one of these criminals comes after you and you shoot him, I'm not going to care too much," he continued. "But if he shoots you, I'm going to be disappointed in you. I'm going to be pissed. You get me?"

Over the years, I'd gotten to know Matt Cook, who is a good friend of our chief operating officer, Barb Visher. Cook was Colorado's first top cop of marijuana. Initially, he believed with a vengeance that legalization was a scam—a way for stoners to get their high on and beat the rap doing it. Over the course of two years, he helped the state set up its enforcement division. He and his colleagues were charged with tracking down instances where legal marijuana product was diverted into the illegal market. They were the ones who checked the manifests, tracking the flow of goods and revenue as it made its way through Colorado's nascent cannabis system.

They got off to a rocky start. At first, they were way behind the rest of us. Everyone who had a dream had opened a dispensary or started a grow while the cops were still trying to hire and train their officers.

But eventually, their growing pains came to an end.

The cops are not our friends but our regulators. Our relationship is a professional one. But those of us who run clean businesses have earned the respect of these officers.

I knew that the tide had turned when I heard that Matt Cook had left the service and had embarked on a highly remunerative business in his retirement.

He was now one of the best-paid national consultants in the legal marijuana business. He traveled around the United States, helping other states set up their legal marijuana enforcement divisions.

Once he hated the thought of legal weed. Now he sees it differently. In the right hands, legal marijuana can be smart business.

7

SEED TO SALE TO BUST

AND JUST AS THINGS WERE GOING GREAT, WE WERE about to go broke again.

Suddenly, every time I went to deliver buds to the dispensaries I had begun to supply, a couple of the owners couldn't pay.

"Where's the money?"

They'd hem and haw and shrug their shoulders. "Sorry," they'd say, "we spent it all on something else."

Now, granted, nearly everyone who leaped into the cannabis industry early did so without adequate start-up money. The near-constant stream of expenses, taxes, and new regulations put a serious burden on a lot of businesses. But this sudden surge in nonpayments felt different.

Apparently, it wasn't bad enough that I was struggling with banks and city bureaucrats, or that everyone I dealt with thought I was single-handedly bringing down modern American culture. Now I was forced to play the role of the heavy in some gangster film: *Where's my fucking money?*

No doubt about it. It was a horrible, tense time, and it was only going to get worse.

What had happened?

Sometimes all it takes to change the ecosystem surrounding an industry is a simple change in the law. In this case, the state of Colorado had decided that all marijuana businesses should be "vertically integrated." That means that if you grew the marijuana, you had to be the one who sold it as well. If you ran a dispensary, you had to sell product you had grown yourself.

On paper, it sounded like a great way to close the loop and decrease the chance that a pound or two of product would go missing and end up in the illegal drug market. What could be simpler? The state regulators would track the buds from *seed to sale.*

The new law was like telling Exxon that it could no longer sell gasoline to the mom-and-pop distributor around the corner. And telling every mom-and-pop gas station that it had to set up its own oil platforms in the North Sea.

Like many growers, we were not in the position to be able to open a dispensary on the fly. We were so focused on growing, on keeping our warehouse greenhouses running smoothly, that we had not the time, the money, or the inclination to get into retail.

But the law said we had to.

Luckily, a solution presented itself. All around the state, growers like us were solving the problem by forming business partnerships with existing retail operations. What could be simpler? You'd draw up a contract and marry the very same people—dispensary owners—who had been buying from you all along.

It made a certain kind of sense. We already knew each other, right? They bought my product. They paid their bills on time. Why shouldn't we just get hitched, and live happily ever after, brothers and sister in bud?

I picked four dispensaries that were my best customers and we drew up papers to become partners. Two of my four partnerships blossomed beautifully. I grew the product, brought it to them on a regular basis, and collected my fee, and they sold it to a rapidly growing clientele. The other two partnerships turned into a nightmare. They kept missing payments to our firm. We filed suit, became embroiled in a legal tussle, and ultimately settled for pennies on the dollar. The process dragged on for several months, a time I'll remember not-so-fondly as the third time we almost lost the business.

I had plenty of time to think about what this fresh disaster had taught me. The most immediate lesson was never go in business with someone you can't trust. The marriage analogy was a strangely apt one: If you can't see eye to eye with someone, if you aren't soul mates of a sort, your balance sheets probably shouldn't be legally joined.

When Mr. Pink and I talked, we were almost always on the same page. If we weren't when we started talking, we were when we finished. We sometimes bickered, we sometimes saw things differently, but what we hoped to accomplish with the business was one and the same thing. In the business sense, we were made for each other.

The other thing I learned during this terrible period was something I always knew but probably needed to learn again and again, though not quite so expensively:

He who controls the source of the product controls the market.

Who earned the most supplying gasoline to the American public—the gas station owner around the corner or Exxon?

Who earned the biggest profits annually—the guy who owns your local liquor store or Budweiser?

Whose balance sheet would you rather have—the owner of your local bottling plant or Coca-Cola's?

Who makes more on that new car sale—the dealership or Ford Motor Company?

Ditto that shiny computer you just bought—your local indie computer dealer or Apple?

This holds true for most businesses. If you're manufacturing the product, you're first in line to make the serious money. Anyone else who comes after you earns a small percentage as a middleman.

I hate lawsuits. Who doesn't? But while I was waiting to get justice, I resolved to nail down what was working in my business. I had chosen a good partner in Mr. Pink. And two of my state-mandated marriages were actually working well.

Two things came out of it that changed the course of our business forever. Going forward, I had to stick to growing the product. It was the strongest part of the business, and the most profitable. But if I wanted to establish a brand that struck a chord with the public, I had to have a retail presence, too. So I worked out a deal to acquire the two dispensaries owned by the partners I got along with—not the ones owned by my legal antagonists. I rebranded those locations under the Green Man Cannabis name.

Through the mergers, I acquired new operating partners: Barb Visher, who would become our chief operating officer, and Audra Richmond, now our senior vice president of human resources. Green Man had become bigger—a team. No longer was it just Mr. Pink and I and my vision. Now we had a group of people who woke up every morning with fire in their bellies to make Green Man win.

As part of our legal settlement, I came to retain the services of a grower, a quick-witted young man named Corey, who had a degree in legal cannabis cultivation. Solely through Corey's efforts, one of my antagonists had landed the most coveted award in our fledgling industry—the Cannabis Cup. The first time I met him, I liked Corey immediately. He came off as a thoughtful man with a good head on his shoulders. Not flighty or erratic. No personality issues. A guy I could get along with.

As it happened, I was in the market for a good grower. Brandon's hours had started to drop, and when I confronted him about it, he admitted his heart just wasn't in it. He liked growing marijuana; he just didn't want to grow someone *else's* marijuana. He wanted to start his own company, doing what I was doing. We parted ways amicably. Kim left my employ shortly after, and one of their assistants had already been running the show for a few weeks.

Our company now had two indoor grows and two retail locations. Thankfully, we now also had one of the best growers in the entire state of Colorado.

I had noticed that every time we brought on a new grower, our yields dropped while he or she brought us up to speed. This happened again under Corey, but he immediately instituted an important change to our system that radically reduced our workflow obligations.

Before Corey, we had been using a hydroponic system that used coconut coir fibers as a growing medium. The roots of our plants were surrounded by those fibers and drew their nourishment from the water and plant food we systematically fed them. There was just one drawback to this method, which you can probably guess if you've ever run your hand over the exterior of a coconut. Those fibers have good heft, resist bacteria, and degrade slowly, but they don't stay wet for long. When we used them, we were obliged to water our plants three times a day.

Corey switched us over to a new medium that consisted of peat moss and perlite. The result was a spongy mixture that drained well but stayed relatively moist. Best of all, we only had to water our plants every three days.

It was time to put the bullshit lawsuits behind us and get back to growing some prime bud. Green Man had not only survived another attack; we had blossomed in the process. The challenge had made us bigger, stronger, and more passionate than ever. By the end of the lawsuit, *I* became a *we* and the result was a diverse group of ganja-preneurs ready to put their hearts into making Green Man Cannabis the premier brand of marijuana in Colorado.

8

THE CANNABIS RANCH

ONE MORNING IN 2014 I DROVE OUT OF DOWNTOWN DEN-
ver with the top down. The road took me east, away from the foothills
of the Rocky Mountains. The strip malls and businesses thinned out,
and the blocks became more sparsely populated. Warehouses and
industrial buildings popped up. I rode along streets lined with chain-
link fences topped with barbed wire. When I got to 40th and Ulster,
the road petered out. I pulled over and killed the engine.

I was parked outside the gates of an airplane salvage yard. A tall,
blue corrugated steel building stood on the other side of a fence. The
fuselages of long-retired planes sat in pieces around the site.

The building sat on 15 acres of land, a lopsided rectangle mostly
covered with weeds and the remains of dilapidated airplanes. Some
were military aircraft dating back to World War II. Others were broken husks of planes that had crashed and now lay around, waiting to
be picked apart for parts.

In the 1960s and '70s, the land had served as a rental car main-
tenance facility. At some point in its history, one of its owners had
installed an underground fuel tank. Another time, a jet fuel storage
tank on the adjacent land had burst into flames, coating the land
with toxic soot. Somewhere under that soil lay decades of industrial

waste buried in a hastily constructed landfill, a sad legacy that spoke of how we humans sometimes treat the earth that is our home.

The land and its tortured history had become part of my plans for the future of our business. When I envisioned the marijuana business I'd be building, I'd been wrestling with two conflicting urges that I'd only recently begun sharing with other people.

One was a problem.

The other was a dream.

The problem was this: From the moment we'd set up shop in the warehouse on South River Platte Drive, it had become obvious to me that the cannabis industry was grossly inefficient. In order to grow our plants inside a cinder-block box, we were forced to replicate what nature does effortlessly. Over the last few years, growers had come and gone, and with each new regime, we had upgraded our equipment. We were now operating with cutting-edge technology. Our warehouses held 350 lights, enough to grow nearly 4,000 plants. We were pushing the envelope, moving beyond my one-light-equals-one-pound rule of thumb to one-and-a-quarter pounds per light, harvesting close to 175 pounds of buds a month.

I loved visiting those rooms.

To walk in in the morning and smell the oxygen-rich air, tinged with just the right hint of moisture, and to smell those flowering buds coming into fragrance was a joyful experience. I was so in love with the *aliveness* of it all. It was much more gratifying than being stuck in the artificial environment of an office.

But I still disliked that those plants were thriving in an artificial environment of our own making. The lights cycled on and off, dousing the plants with precisely twelve hours of light and twelve hours of darkness. The plants were surrounded by intake valves and air handlers and air conditioners. The high-pressure sodium lights got so hot that we had set up a separate system to flush out heat. Even the "air" those plants breathed—the carbon dioxide—was supplied by giant tanks that we wheeled in and out for that very purpose. With all the clicking and whirring, it may not have resembled an office, but it did sometimes feel like a factory.

Yes, we got great product this way, but I couldn't help thinking there was a better way. A more natural way. But every time I talked to expert growers, they told me that this was the only way to get great yields.

I didn't understand that, because all over the world commercial growers were growing hothouse crops in glass greenhouses. They used the free power of the sun when they could and cracked open windows to allow the free exchange of air and carbon dioxide. *Their* plants seemed to be doing just fine.

It reminded me of a story.

Once there was a woman who used to bake a ham on holidays and special family occasions. Before she dressed the ham and popped it in the oven, she sliced it in half. Year in and year out, her children watched her do this and always wondered about her culinary technique. Did each half of the ham cook more thoroughly that way? Finally, one day, one of her grown children finally asked her why she did it that way. "I don't know," was her response. "That's the way my mother did it."

In a sense, that's what the best minds on cannabis cultivation were saying. They grew inside cinder-block boxes because that's the way it had always been done. The collective wisdom of the community said this was the best way. But that wisdom dated to a time when the most expert growers were criminals trying to evade the law. It didn't make sense to grow that way anymore.

We were legal now. It was time to come out of the closet.

Doing so would save us money. It still cost us about $850 to grow a pound of marijuana. If we transitioned to a more natural system, I estimated we could probably get the cost down to $350 a pound—nearly a 60 percent decrease in cost. At that rate, we could charge customers less in our dispensaries and still hit the same profit margin. Conceptually, we would be able to sell to our customers and make money for less than our competitors could even grow their product for. If I was wrong, we would lose big on a very expensive gamble. But if I was right, this model would revolutionize the industry so thoroughly that every large indoor grow would eventually become economically obsolete.

But there were also reasons beyond cost and efficiency. It made sense to me that we'd want to share the cannabis industry with the world. We'd want to stop hiding and start demystifying marijuana for people who were curious about it but afraid to try it. If we could show off a modern, large-scale legal marijuana grow facility and educate people about the product and the brand, it would set Green Man apart.

How could I best share our product with the world?

Get it out in the open was the answer. Get it where they can see it. Offer them tours of your facilities. Get them to get acquainted with Green Man in an environment that was fun and familiar, an environment designed with tourists in mind.

Every year, millions of people visited wineries and breweries the world over. People knew exactly what that experience entailed. They took a little tour. They saw the fermentation tanks. They heard brewers and vintners talk about their work. They visited the gift shop afterward and sampled some of the wares. It was a great experience that had done much to educate Americans about wine and had fostered the growth of the microbrewery industry.

Why couldn't we do the same with marijuana?

If we were too shy to do such a thing, if we were too scared of the backlash of sharing a formerly criminal drug with the world in such a way, then weren't we tacitly agreeing that there was something shameful about our product?

The idea for the Cannabis Ranch took root in my imagination and blossomed when I first got into the business. At first, I didn't share it with too many people. I talked to Mr. Pink about my concept, and though he was enthusiastic, we both realized that it would be a while before we could make the dream happen. At the time, the industry was geared solely toward medical marijuana patients. The only people who could enter a dispensary had to be bearers of a red card. Building an expensive tourist destination for so small an audience was impractical.

But when Colorado voters approved recreational marijuana in 2012, it made sense to start thinking big. That's when I hired the architect to create a conceptual model and drawings so I could more clearly communicate the dream to others.

In strictest confidence, I shared the concept with Dax, my real estate buddy, who got to work looking for the ideal parcel of land. Whenever I had some time, we'd drive all over the region looking at places that we thought would work. I was picky about finding the right place. I wanted a location that would be highly visible and accessible from Denver International Airport (DIA). I wanted it to be in the city and county of Denver, because it had become the most accommodating to ganjapreneurs like me.

I suppose I could have looked for property outside Denver, but I'd watched other cannabis businesses plunk their cash on land and warehouses outside of town, only to later run afoul of county zoning commissions. The four surrounding counties still didn't look kindly on marijuana, no matter how legal it was in the state.

No, if I was going to do this, I would have to stay in Denver, which was still marijuana friendly.

This wasn't the first time I'd come by to see the airplane graveyard. I'd come out the first time with the realtors and had been back several more times to see it on my own. I had a few other parcels in mind, but this was the one that kept reeling me in.

I'd been talking with a businessman from out of town who was keen to invest in the marijuana industry. I met more of these people as the years went by and our business flourished. These days it was tough to find decent investments, especially if you were a man or woman with a billion to your name.

This guy—whom I'll call William—had been saddened to learn that his out-of-state residency meant that he was ineligible to own stock in a Colorado cannabis company. The state had enacted such a rule to keep the inevitable rush from outsiders at bay. But I had thought of a way that William could help us out. If he was game, he could buy this sad little property, build the facility we needed, and rent it to us for twenty years. It was win-win all around. He'd get the 15-plus percent his portfolio demanded, and he'd get a ringside seat at the table in the cannabis industry. Someday, when the ban on out-of-staters was lifted, maybe he'd be able to invest directly in the marijuana operating company.

I just needed to get him interested in taking a chance on the property. That wouldn't be easy. The airplane graveyard was near Interstate 70, the main artery leading in and out of downtown Denver, and it wasn't far from DIA. But the land was hardly a pristine agricultural site.

This place certainly had some environmental issues. Engineers I'd spoken to had said that the section of land atop the landfill would probably sink seven inches over the next twenty years, as the contents of the landfill settled.

But all was not lost. It *was* possible to salvage a good chunk of the property. The land would cost about $3.2 million, and I'd estimated another $800,000 for environmental cleanup and remediation. We could show the world that it was possible to do some good with an injured piece of land and in a sense atone for our own resource-intensive industry.

I wasn't planning to plant marijuana directly in the soil. Those precious plants would spend their lives in 5-pound bags of growing medium, just the way we grew them in our warehouse. But I did need the space on the site to construct a greenhouse to enclose them.

As I peered through the chain-link fence now, I tried to imagine just where the greenhouse would go. Once it was built, anyone driving on I-70 toward Denver would see it rising two stories into the air.

If you flew into Denver from the sky, you'd spy it out the window of your aircraft. Wouldn't that be a fine way to get people's attention? Wouldn't that make people curious?

Recently, Denver's Regional Transportation District had made a decision that made this parcel of land even more desirable. It had announced the extension of a light-rail line that would run from the airport straight into town. Three stops in, the light rail would stop at Smith Road and Ulster Street, right at the end of the block where I was standing.

It sounded too good to be true.

It practically made me laugh to think about it. As it was, the state's airports were strictly off-limits for marijuana. Since recreational marijuana became legal, the state was happy to have travelers come experience Colorado's exciting new cannabis culture. Come, smoke, get joyfully stoned was the message. But don't even think of smuggling some of that weed onto an airplane on the way out of town. The city of Colorado Springs had even installed "amnesty boxes" at its airport. As people headed back to the real world, they were encouraged to drop their extra weed in one of these green boxes, no questions asked.

I kept thinking about those travelers at DIA. Some of them never left the airport because they had to catch connecting flights. If our Cannabis Ranch was close by, was it so crazy to envision savvy travelers booking long layovers at DIA so they could catch the light-rail system straight to our front door? They could ride out, take the tour, get stoned, have lunch in our restaurant, get stoned again, and ride the train back to catch their flight.

The idea was so enticing, I couldn't wait.

I checked my watch. It was time to run out and pick up William. He and his advisor, Justin, were coming back to town to look at this deal again; they'd been out a few times already. They weren't landing at DIA but rather a private airport in Centennial, Colorado. I'd be waiting on the tarmac for them when their company jet pulled to a stop. I'd give them a warm welcome, then whisk them away for lunch to talk over the deal some more, then out to the site again.

Business deals of this kind are a little like courtship. You both want it to happen, but you're always wary. It has to feel right, and the numbers have to work.

I wanted to get this thing built badly. But creating the first of anything is never easy.

9

FAMILY: HAGESETH; GENUS: *CANNABIS*

MY WIFE AND I WERE MEETING MY OLDEST DAUGHTER'S
teacher for the first time on the night of parent–teacher conferences.
The teacher leaned forward and said in a low voice: "Before we get
started, do you mind my asking you a question? What do each of you
do for a living?"

I could see where this was going.

My wife fidgeted. She was nervous. She had not yet come to
terms with my business.

"It's just . . ." The teacher paused. "Your daughter said the other
day in class that her daddy grows plants. When I asked her what kind
of plants her daddy grew . . . well . . . she said . . . *marijuana*."

"That is true," I said. "I'm in the medical marijuana business. I
grow in a large warehouse and do it legally. I don't grow at home."

Just because you know what you do for a living doesn't mean
everyone around you can explain it. I was beginning to realize that
the people closest to me—my family—were struggling with a variety
of conflicting feelings about my line of work.

I thought I'd prepared well for this. When I first got into the
cannabis industry, I made an effort to read as much as I could about

marijuana. I wanted to be as educated as possible. I knew there would be questions from family members. A few in my family are deeply religious. After a lifetime of associating marijuana with sin, they might be troubled by my new venture. So I read up, I studied, I thought hard about my reasons for choosing this life. I wanted to be able to answer their questions in a loving and considered way.

Of course, that started with my children. I wanted them to grow up as healthy, responsible members of society. When they asked about my work, I gave it to them straight. Marijuana was a product that adults used to relax, not unlike alcohol and something like cigarettes. Yes, our state had legalized marijuana as medicine, but at the time we were speaking, it was available for sale only to adults over twenty-one who had demonstrated medical need.

I also watched what sort of language I used. I didn't want them to hear a lot of limiting messages when they were growing up. *Don't do this. Don't do that. Watch out for that.* That sort of language only made kids afraid of the world. I'd prefer that they knew what *all* these vices were capable of doing to people, so they'd be better able to make good choices.

For example, I hoped that I'd be able to raise daughters who were strong enough to say no to drugs like cocaine or heroin. I hoped that those substances would strike them as highly addictive, dangerous, and capable of killing them via overdose.

There are certainly issues surrounding marijuana use and adolescents. There's evidence, for example, that marijuana may impair growing minds and bodies. But if one of my daughters was moved to experiment with marijuana someday, I think I'd be thankful that she wasn't getting addicted to nicotine or messing with alcohol. Teens on alcohol have just enough courage and bravado to do something stupid. In less than an hour, they're capable of making a string of bad decisions that will haunt them for the rest of their lives. I'm not denying that there have been stoned adolescents and adults who have, say, gotten behind the wheel of a car. But if your kid is toking in the basement with friends, some of the most *likely* outcomes are that they will watch a ton of movies on Netflix, have a mind-blowing realization, laugh a lot, order in a pizza, clean their entire room, or pass out on the couch.

I think parents who have some experience with marijuana understand this. I get in these kinds of exuberant arguments with people all the time. "Look," I recently told a group of moms, "say your kids are out for the night. They have a bottle of Jack Daniel's or a bag of weed, and they are going to use one of them. Which would you rather have them do?"

Hands down, the moms all said marijuana.

I don't think that kind of response would have been possible in the 1930s, during the days of *Reefer Madness.* Parents back then would not have had enough personal experience with the drug to know that there was a difference. They would have bought the government-backed party line that marijuana would drive their children insane and compel them to commit murder.

I suppose we can all be grateful that so many adults these days have smoked marijuana. It's making them better parents. Not necessarily more tolerant, mind you, just more educated and realistic.

As you may have guessed from our talk with my daughter's teacher, my wife was still uncomfortable with the notion of her husband being in the marijuana business. She was intrigued that the law was changing. She was interested in how such a decision would impact her home state. But she didn't want her husband in the business, let alone smoking the stuff. She'd grown up in a fairly conservative Colorado family.

"I am not telling my parents what you're doing," she told me early on. "It'll just upset them."

Well, I expected that. But as the months passed and I was struggling with those first few harvests, I lost track of time on the home front. It was getting awfully close to the holidays.

"Look," I said, "you have to tell them *something.* We're going to see them for Christmas!"

Well, she did. The news went over like a lead balloon. A big, ol' marijuana-tainted lead balloon. The holidays were tense. And by the following Easter, her crusty dad got up the nerve to ask me a single question during our time together. "So—how's that pot thing going?"

Interestingly, my experience with my own parents was remarkably different. I suppose you could say that we have become a closer family because of marijuana.

How is that possible? Well, I said earlier that the story of marijuana policy in this country is a little like the personal evolution of a human being. We form opinions, we enact rigid policies, we suffer consequences because of those policies, and we relent and grow to a higher state of being. I'd argue that both of my parents went through those phases.

My dad, for example, recently had a life-changing experience. A friend of his in South Dakota had a grandson who suffered from a lifetime of intractable seizures. This grandfather reached out to my dad after seeing Dr. Sanjay Gupta's report on CNN that touted the medical aspects of marijuana and focused on a little girl with symptoms similar to those of his grandson. My dad suggested his friend begin reading up on cannibidiol (CBD) tinctures to see if this marijuana-derived product might be worth trying on the friend's grandson.

Most people never look past tetrahydrocannabinol (THC), the psychoactive compound in marijuana that gives humans that high. But THC belongs to a larger family of compounds found in marijuana called cannabinoids. One of the other compounds is CBD, and it has become recognized in recent years for its ability to treat numerous conditions, including pediatric epilepsy. There's no high associated with taking CBD. It's usually administered as an oral liquid formulation.

As I write this, a drug made with this compound has been granted orphan drug status with the Food and Drug Administration and is slated for clinical trials. "Orphan diseases" are ones that affect an extremely small percentage of the human population, so small that it often doesn't pay for a drug company to invest its resources in developing treatments for them. One incentive the U.S. government offers drug companies is the ability to fast-track the development of these designated "orphan drugs."

In the South Dakota case, the grandfather was able to research CBD and talk it over with his family. They decided to buy some CBD and try it out on the boy. The child, who had had fifteen to twenty seizures every day since doctors discovered a tumor in his brain when he was only three, began taking the CBD tincture. After ten days of taking the tincture, the grandson went seven days without having a single seizure. Those were the first seizure-free days in his young life. After a month of taking the tincture, the absence of seizures allowed the grandson to resume a regular life. As I write this, he is getting ready to begin home schooling for the first time.

Emboldened by his friend's story, my father began immersing himself more enthusiastically in the medical literature surrounding marijuana.

BECAUSE OF MY BUSINESS EXPERIENCE, I'm often asked for financial advice by friends and family. Shortly after I got started in the marijuana business, I got an urgent call from a longtime friend that I'll call Bruce. "Can I come by to talk with you? It's kind of important."

"Sure," I said. We made a date, and I put it out of my mind.

He showed up a few days later, and I could tell when he came in the door that he was agitated. Papers tucked under his arm. Concern in his eyes. "Is there someplace private we can talk? I think we're going to need a computer."

I led him into my office and closed the door. He started opening his files and laying sheets of paper on my desk. Tons of financials from his current living situation. His bank statements. His house. The car. Everything.

"Are you having money problems?"

"I think so," he said with a sigh.

We started working on a spreadsheet together, and as we did, he loosened up a little and started to talk.

"All we need is about $3,000 a month," he said, "if we sell the house to live comfortably in a senior community. But how long can we make it last at that expense?"

"You're gonna move?"

"I don't have a choice, I don't think. Look at the numbers."

I looked and fiddled and clicked around. I love spreadsheets. They're the quickest way I know of drilling down to the facts of any financial situation. As the rows and columns click into place with every little change you make, you start internalizing the numbers, seeing patterns, and you can get a sense which numbers are the most critical.

"You know," I said, "you're barely seventy and you guys are still in good health. I don't think you need to move out."

"It's just tough coming up with the money."

I clicked around. Sifted through his papers.

"You're telling me you need $3,000 a month," I said, "but what I'm seeing is, if you can come up with *$3,600* a month, you can keep the car and the house and you don't have to move anywhere. Your life stays exactly the same."

"Sounds fine, but where's the money coming from?"

At the time he had Social Security, a retirement account that had been decimated by the market crash, and a part-time job that he enjoyed.

It was obvious to me what he should do. But I knew it would be a struggle to get him to accept it.

"You know what I do for a living, right?"

"Marijuana. I know. What's that got to do with anything?"

I smiled. "Have you ever considered growing pot?"

His face changed. He looked disgusted. His head was shaking even before I could get another word out.

"Hear me out."

"That's ridiculous."

"Bruce, you can do this. It's not rocket science."

"I'm not growing marijuana."

And here he went into a long diatribe. He admired what I was doing in my business. He wasn't against marijuana per se, now that it was legal, but setting up shop to grow it seemed like taking this legal pot business a little too far.

"Are you saying I should come work for you?"

"No—I'm saying get yourself some lights and set up shop in your basement."

He was silent for a little while.

I have no idea what he was thinking. Maybe he was considering how I'd been willing to take the risk. Maybe some part of him was tuning in to the obvious joy I was having at the helm of a new business. If I could do it—

"How would I even do that? I'm not skilled at . . . at *that*."

"I can teach you. You'll grow as a Caregiver. You'll grow specifically for patients who you will then sell it to. That part is all legal. You have a good head on your shoulders. You'll figure the rest out, and I can help."

He was shaking his head again.

"It's completely legal, and you'll make decent money."

He went silent again.

Thinking.

Eyes roving over the papers.

Thinking.

After a long while he shrugged. "How much money are we talking?"

I WOULDN'T WANT TO GIVE the impression that it's difficult to grow marijuana in your home. Certainly millions of people do just that all over the world, often illegally. It's the same old story: If you want to keep your illegal activity a secret, you grow your plants in a place that's out of sight.

Now it was legal in Colorado.

But that doesn't mean it was a cinch. If he was going to do this right, Bruce would need lights, fans, and a dedicated air conditioner. He would need some instruction in the finer points of plant nutrition and cultivation. He would need to quiet his negativity and learn to be a good student again.

He would read and take notes and talk to my growers and see what he could pick up on his own. I was hoping to "teach a man to fish" rather than giving him a fish.

One of the hard things for home growers to realize is that once you go down this path, you must be committed. It's not like sprinkling a few houseplants around the house and then going about your business, occasionally missing a few waterings here and there.

No—if you're gonna grow, you have to expect that it's like supervising a child or a couple of pets. They must be fed. They must be watered. Their environment must be carefully monitored. And you must do this every single day.

It wasn't long before Bruce's basement was fragrant with the smell of ripening buds. I walked him through his first harvest and had the privilege of sharing his delight when he delivered that harvest to local dispensaries. I watched as he counted up his earnings.

He was incredulous. "Five *thousand* dollars?"

It wasn't going to be easy. It's tough work. But needless to say, his money problems were over. He and his wife were able to continue living in their home. They were happy and relieved. The crisis had passed.

But that wasn't the end of it. Now, every time I ran into Bruce, he nattered on about some new method of marijuana cultivation that he'd found on the Internet. Or something he had read in a book. Or gleaned from a conversation with the guy in his local grow store.

Suddenly, the guy who was afraid to build his own home grow was an expert. He had learned to fish.

MEANWHILE, MY MOTHER had been struggling with a problem of her own that was not so easily solved. Her boyfriend, Bob, had been diagnosed with liver cancer and given about three months to live.

Bob was a kind and open-minded man, and my mother had always been supportive of all my business ventures, including my marijuana business. So I wasn't surprised when she broached the subject of Bob possibly using some marijuana to alleviate the symptoms associated with his chemotherapy.

Sad to say, chances are high you know of someone who has undergone this type of treatment. In the United States, one in four people will battle cancer in their lifetime. Not everyone who undergoes chemo experiences side effects, but many do. Those effects range from loss of appetite, nausea, and difficulty sleeping to hair loss, fingernail loss, loss of sensation in the extremities, and many more. Cancer patients typically take additional medications to manage these symptoms. They might use sleeping pills and antinausea meds, for example, to combat problems brought on by the chemo. This is a common pattern with modern medicine: We're prescribed one medication to treat our disease and a host of other meds to treat the symptoms brought on by that medication. The pills-on-top-of-pills pattern is so ubiquitous that no one seems to question it anymore.

Anytime I hear an idiot politician or media pundit dismiss medical marijuana legalization as a ploy to give stoners their plaything, I cringe. If I could point to one disease that hastened the adoption of medical marijuana in this country, I'd point to cancer. These people are suffering, and marijuana helps. A lot. I'm proud that we're finally waking up to the therapeutic power of this little plant.

Now, yes, you will find plenty of activists who argue that marijuana can in fact treat or cure cancer. I'm not going to go there. I'm not a physician. I'm not a scientist. But I will say that numerous scientific journal articles observe that cannabinoids—the active compounds in marijuana—have displayed cancer-fighting properties in lab experiments. They have been shown to impact various types of cancers, from brain and breast cancers to those afflicting the pancreas, lungs, and others. In studies where scientists have investigated the health of marijuana smokers and of non–marijuana smokers, the marijuana smokers have been found to have lower incidences of cancer. But let's say you don't believe the claims that marijuana's cannabinoids can zap tumors. Let's say you insist the drug deserves closer study. Fine.

Many of our customers find marijuana helps them with the simple things. It kills pain. It's a powerful anti-inflammatory. It helps reduce spasms and convulsions in people with epilepsy. It's a bronchodilator that helps patients with asthma breathe better. It chases away nausea. Marijuana's legendary ability to give you the munchies becomes lifesaving if chemotherapy has decimated your desire to eat a decent meal. Marijuana's high banishes feelings of sadness. Its power as a relaxant allows many users to get a good night's sleep.

Part of the secret of its power lies in the design of the human brain. In the 1990s, Israeli scientists found that humans have special receptors in their brains that allow them to interact with and process

THC and other cannabinoids. Why do we have those receptors? you ask. The answer is that the human body routinely manufactures its *own* CBDs—called *endo*cannabinoids (eCBs). I'm simplifying things immensely, but it turns out that the eCB system is our body's way of protecting our nerve cells from becoming overexcited. To quote marijuana horticulture expert Ed Rosenthal from his famous *Marijuana Grower's Handbook,* "The eCBs act as negative feedback, to say, 'Whoa! That's enough input, now slow down!'"

One of the cannabinoids our body makes is called anandamide, which some scientists have dubbed the "brain's own marijuana," though that term is admittedly simplistic. The first part of the word *ananda*mide comes from the Sanskrit word for "bliss," which is why anandamide is sometimes also called "the bliss molecule." (Anandamide is found naturally in our brains—and in foods like chocolate.) Clearly, the eCB system is all about protecting the body, modulating our immune responses, and generating our feel-good responses.

The science on this is compelling, deserving of further research. Yet researchers lament that they are frequently denied federal permission to study marijuana's effects. It's weird. Marijuana does all this *good* yet the United States has focused obsessively on the fact that weed gets people high. If the government truly believed that's all marijuana was good for, it would have a leg to stand on.

But the truth is, it knows better. Few people realize that the government itself actually holds a patent for medicinal use of cannabinoids. Or that the feds grow medical marijuana for research and compassionate use on their own farm in Oxford, Mississippi. And yet the government continues to lock down marijuana nationwide as a Schedule I drug, claiming that it is of no redeeming medical value. Instead, it prefers to allow large pharmaceutical companies to develop artificial cannabinoid products, which the government classifies as Schedule III drugs, those that have some medical use.

That bias speaks volumes. Doctors have a preference for easily quantified doses that can be administered orally or injected. They become nervous when someone says they just want to smoke a plant. How will that patient control the dosage? How will they know how much of the active ingredient they've taken? Those are legitimate questions, but at the same time, we can't ignore that fact that patients who use marijuana often can reduce the dosages of all those supporting medications they're taking to combat their side effects.

So I felt my mom was on solid ground proposing that Bob smoke a little weed. But he wasn't having it. He was a conservative Colorado plainsman. He didn't smoke tobacco, let alone marijuana.

You know what? I get it. Like the cop who stopped me in the Safeway parking lot, Bob had spent his life under a system that said marijuana was wrong. When his elected officials and local police talked about putting away drug users, citizens like Bob couldn't help but agree. Guys like Bob were law-abiding; marijuana smokers were criminals. Being a law-abiding citizen is a powerful part of many people's identity. You don't just shuck that belief system off because you're dying of a terrible disease.

So I think we have to applaud people who come around to trying what they have spent their lives avoiding. Bob tried marijuana. My mom, his caretaker during this time, set him up with a glass pipe and some weed, and showed him what to do.

Bob tried. It just didn't work for him. He didn't like the smoke and the coughing sensation that went with it.

"I can't do this," he told her.

Smoking is the time-honored way to ingest marijuana, but it's not the only way. In recent years, the industry has promoted vaporizers as a safer alternative. Vaporizers heat up the THC resins to the point where they become airborne. You then breathe the resulting mist. Vaporizers neatly sidestep the biggest issue of smoking: burning plant material.

Smoking marijuana is not nearly as dangerous as smoking tobacco. That's because to get their hit of nicotine, people are obliged to smoke numerous cigarettes and thus inhale a ton of tars that are the products of tobacco leaf combustion. Marijuana smokers tend to smoke less than tobacco users because marijuana is more potent. Some doctors have observed that one hit of a joint with a THC level of the patient's own choosing might be enough to banish that patient's nausea for several hours—and stimulate their appetite to boot. You don't need much to do the trick.

But my mom thought a vaporizer would be too complicated for Bob to operate. She thought of something else: edibles.

I told you earlier that marijuana seeds have served as a nutrient-rich food for thousands of years. If you had visited certain drugstores in the United States in the 1860s, you probably would have been able to find "hasheesh candy," described as a "pleasurable and harmless stimulant." Such products disappeared when cannabis was banned in the 1930s. Edibles didn't get a boost again until the appearance of the classic pot brownie in a 1954 cookbook by Alice B. Toklas.

But ye olde pot brownie is almost passé these days. You wouldn't believe the sheer variety of edibles out there. There isn't a marijuana dispensary in the country that doesn't offer hard candies, chocolate bars, gummy chews, cookies, drinks, colas, mints—you name it. You can also buy tinctures, oils, and butters that incorporate buds so you can go home and cook or bake your own concoction.

It's a brave new world of flavor, taste, and recipes. There's just one caveat: You've got to go easy on the edibles. When you're smoking, you know after one hit or two how the THC is affecting you. Your lungs pump that active ingredient into your bloodstream almost immediately. If you feel a strong high coming on, you can lay off the toking. If you feel that particular strain is too strong for you, you can choose a product with a lower THC level next time. But with edibles, you won't feel the THC until the food product is digested in your stomach and sent to your bloodstream. You could easily eat too much marijuana and have a bad experience. We in the industry owe it to our customers to standardize the amount of THC in each serving to solve this problem.

My mom played it safe with Bob. One night she presented him with a couple of lollipops. Her instructions were simple. Suck on one and wait. See what impact it has on you. Don't take another today.

Well, he quickly fell into a fine routine. He sucked on one lollipop immediately after each chemo session and found that it helped reduce his anxiety and helped him sleep. The following morning, he'd suck on another to quell any resulting queasiness and boost his appetite. He also found that he could get by on fewer painkillers, which had unpleasant side effects. He used lollipops as needed to treat himself for pain and nausea.

Bob's three-month life sentence turned into twenty months. When he died in 2011, I was sad for my mom and mourned his passing with his many friends and family. I admired him for a number of reasons, but I especially admired his courage in trying something he once so adamantly opposed.

10

BEST IN SHOW

I'M PROBABLY THE ONLY CHIEF EXECUTIVE IN THE COUN-try, possibly the world, who will offer to let you smoke out of one of the awards that decorate his retail space.

When people visit, their gaze inevitably takes in the object that sits in a glass enclosure in our downtown Denver location. The glass trophy is about a foot tall, with a depression on the top and two glass necks extending from the central chamber. It's a beautiful piece of handmade glassware. The words etched into the side read: *Colorado Cup, Best Sativa 2012.* It will always be special to me for two reasons: It's the first award our company ever won. And it's a working bong.

How we won it—and how we started racking up awards for our cannabis products—is really a story about feedback.

All companies crave feedback. Most often it comes from customers. And some of those moments can be poignant as well. I know of one customer, an elderly woman in her seventies, who comes into our shop all the time to buy marijuana to help her with the pain she suffers from a debilitating muscular disease. She is always accompanied by her husband, who is a nonsmoker. But the two of them have become fixtures at our downtown location on Denver's Santa Fe Drive. When I was visiting recently, the woman made a point of coming over to me and telling me how well she was being treated by one of our budtenders, Jen.

At first glance, you would not think the two women had much in common. One's an elderly woman who moves with difficulty. The other is a hip, healthy young woman covered with tattoos and piercings. But they have found common ground in their passion for marijuana. What started as a simple transaction has blossomed into a weekly ritual.

That's a beautiful kind of feedback that every business owner needs to hear and see. It reaffirms that you're creating a business—a culture and an environment—where all kinds of people feel welcome.

But if we're honest, entrepreneurs have to admit that we also crave feedback from our peers. We want people in our own industries to nod and say we've done a great job.

The marijuana industry may have been new in the United States, but now that it was out of the closet in a few states, it was losing no time organizing competitions. Our grow program had blossomed under Corey's leadership. Our harvests were back on track. Our confidence was growing. It was only inevitable that we would start to think about entering some of these new cannabis contests. *Rooster Magazine,* Colorado's edgiest arts monthly, was sponsoring something it called the Colorado Cup. There was no fancy exhibition attached to the competition. There would be no award ceremony. No partylike atmosphere in one of the state's convention centers. All we had to do was submit our entries—the best of our best weed—and wait to be notified.

Rather than a small group of us conducting a selection process at the office, we hit upon the idea of throwing a private strain selection party off the premises. That way, all our card-carrying guests would feel free to smoke in a relaxed setting, get high, and identify the strains they thought we should enter. It sounded like a great idea for a party. Naturally, we made sure to hire caterers who brought plenty of food.

You wouldn't believe the debates people would get into over marijuana. It's not enough when you're doing a selection to say, "Well, this weed got me high, so I'm giving it a thumbs-up!"

It's a little more complicated than that. I'll go back to the beer analogy I used earlier. Say you're the owner of a local microbrewery who does a great business in your neck of the woods selling IPA— India pale ale—to your customers. You're so proud of your beer that you decide to enter it in one of the million beer competitions that occur every year in the United States. You do okay, but you don't win. In fact, afterward, someone close to the judges pulls you over to give you some pointers. "Yours is a great beer," the guy says, "but it's not totally representative of an IPA."

This observation—*close but no cigar*—is probably heard wherever aficionados gather to judge the merits of whatever their passions are: beer, wine, chocolates, mustards, classic cars, and on and on. I'll bet right now there's someone who just lost a dog show who is hearing a similar thing: "Your schnauzer was wonderful, Mrs. Jones. She just wasn't the *quintessential* schnauzer. The *ideal* schnauzer. She didn't hit the *benchmark* all schnauzers must hit to be considered perfect." There are subtle variations that creep into any product—or breed—that differentiate it from the standard. You might enjoy and celebrate those differences locally, but when it comes time to enter a competition, you have to nail the standard.

So the night of that selection party, as the haze grew and perfumed every corner of my house, people were debating the merits of our weed on this level. This is an awesome Super Lemon Haze, they were saying, but is it so typical of the Super Lemon Haze strain that the judges will love it? Did it have that taste of a smoky lemon meringue pie when you smoked it? Did those buds have that clean scent of lemon peel when you sniffed it in your hand? Because if not, let's pick a different strain.

And they'd pass around containers of different strains and smoke small samples of each from a little glass pipe or a bong.

Round and round we'd go. Those of us who weren't blasted out of our minds or absolutely giddy took some notes on the process. Come morning, we had our guests' written comments on every strain, and we made some decisions in the light of day. We filled out our application, assembled our samples, and dropped everything off at the location the magazine sponsoring the contest had designated.

And we promptly forgot about it.

We had a business to run. We couldn't waste time waiting by the phone.

Corey and I had become friends since he'd started working for us. I enjoyed hanging out with him and his family. Since there was no space to meet at the grow facilities, he and I had grown accustomed to hitting a local bar, El Diablo, where we'd hash out our plans over shots of chilled Patrón tequila and Dos Equis beer.

On one such afternoon I said, "Hey, what's the deal with the Colorado Cup? Shouldn't we have heard by now?"

We called the magazine the next day and got hold of the guy who had launched the contest. I could imagine what a great time the judges of this particular competition must have had working their way through the glorious abundance of weed that had poured into their office from every grower in the state. Their judging process had to have been ten thousand times more fragrant and hysterical than the selection party at my house.

The guy sounded like he was still coming down from that high.

"Oh, yeah!" he said. "I was gonna call you guys! You won!"

Actually, we won not one but three awards. Our Super Lemon Haze had come in third place for best sativa. Our Hells Angels OG Kush had come in third for best indica. The stunner: Our Jack Herer had taken first place for best sativa in the state.

The next day the magazine dropped off the glass trophy/bong at our downtown store. It had been hand-blown by an artisanal glass business, Kind Creations, in Fort Collins.

All of us were ecstatic. Holy shit, I thought, three years of this crazy business and it's finally paying off. The money was good. We were hitting our numbers, the company was operating smoothly, and we were getting great feedback from our customers. But this was something different. Outside recognition was hugely gratifying.

We were on the map!

Granted, the map extended only to the borders of our very square state, but we were on it just the same.

When the magazine issue touting our victory appeared, the publisher dropped off plenty of copies to share with employees and customers.

And then just a few days later, a couple of angry Hells Angels members walked into our downtown Denver dispensary.

Since it's probably been a while since you rode with a motorcycle crew, let me fill you in. Shortly after our budtenders opened shop that morning, in walked two burly biker dudes in "cuts"—black leather vests emblazoned with patches signifying their membership. On the other side of the glass door, my employees could see yet another biker waiting outside, his arms crossed as if blocking the door. As I've mentioned, you can't enter a medical marijuana dispensary unless you're a card-carrying patient. So I suppose I should be grateful that these two fellows were following the law.

The two men flashed their red medical marijuana cards and held up the magazine article I just mentioned. "It says in here that you guys sell the Hells Angels OG Kush. Is that right?"

"Uh . . . yeah?"

"Can we see it?"

My clerk, after checking them into our system, led them down the bar to a jar and showed them the buds.

There's a lot of marijuana history in that name. The strain is said to have been originally bred by Hells Angels members themselves. It became legendary, with wonderful scent of cotton candy and pine. We grew this bud in 2013, and it tested at more than 33 percent

THC—higher amounts of THC than any bud entered in competition, ever. As my budtenders tell our customers, it comes on like a freight train. It'll pretty much erase anything you're feeling—from stress to excruciating pain. The OG in the name has a mysterious origin. Some insist it refers to a now-defunct, Canadian-based marijuana website—Overgrown.com—and honors those pioneers who traded seeds and kept great strains alive, albeit illegally, until the Canadian government shut them down under pressure from the United States. Still others say that OG stands for "Original Gangster," in honor of an early strain that was big in Southern California, or for "Ocean Grown," because it was bred near the California coast. Either way, OG has come to signify a classic strain. And Kush refers to a major mountain chain that bridges India and Pakistan, where marijuana is thought to have originated.

The leaves of the OG Kush have a very distinctive "frosted" look, almost as if the leaf has sprouted a furry coat. If you look closely, you can see that the tiny hairs that give the bud that look actually secrete sticky resins. These structures are called trichomes. Dried buds will also have flecks of tan, light green, and dark green, which, combined with that piney resin smell, can pretty much persuade you that you're looking at the real Hells Angels OG Kush.

"Okay," one of the bikers said. "That's it, all right. We're putting you on notice right now that you need to immediately cease and desist from using our name or logo in any capacity. It is protected by copyright. If you fail to comply, you will receive a letter from our attorney. We will file a suit to protect our trademark."

One of my employees gave me a call.

"Wait," I said. "You've gotta be fucking kidding me. The Hells Angels are threatening us with a trademark violation suit?"

"They say we can still sell it, but we can't use their name!"

It was the most absurd thing I've ever heard of. The sort of exchange you'd expect to see in a comedy sketch on the TV show *Portlandia*.

I had read that the Angels had started cracking down on people and businesses that used their name and logo. I don't blame them. There are too many people in this world who glom onto any design or product to project to the world that they are cool. The Hells Angels mark was one of the most abused, in that respect. When we started growing and selling that particular indica, I thought we were honoring its history in the cannabis community by continuing to label it under its original name.

But okay. We had received their special brand of feedback, and we were ready to acquiesce to their request. From that moment forward, the product took on a new name: Hells OG Kush. It's still there in our dispensaries. Just don't ask for it by the old moniker. You don't want to piss those guys off.

I WAS SITTING IN A BUSINESS MEETING in the middle of the day, smoking some weed, taking notes, and loving my life.

In my old life, business meetings were a necessary evil. I had several a day. They appeared on my calendar, and I marched through them like an automaton, trying to cover as much ground as possible. Meet some new people. Make some decisions. Close some deals. Inevitably I'd get stuck in a dog of a meeting where whoever was running the show wasn't keeping his charges on task. The meetings dragged on. My eyes glazed over. I was bored out of my mind.

In my new life, meetings were joyful events. Corey would sometimes show up with some fantastic new product. As with any business, a new product means a host of new decisions. How does this fit into our line? Does it have any special features we ought to call out in our marketing? How did it do in the grow? Was it an eight-week strain, or longer or shorter than that benchmark? Did we get 1 pound per light in the grow room, more or less? What are we telling our customers about it? How will it help the medical customers? And the biggest question of all: What's it like to smoke?

There was only one way to know.

I've always had a high tolerance for THC. I can smoke plenty of weed without becoming debilitated. When I was still in my twenties and starting my first ice cream business, I'd smoke in the back room to get ready for the day or when we were closing up at night. When I was running my real estate company, I'd smoke on my time—never in the office, never around clients or others I imagined wouldn't approve.

But all that's changed in my new life. At one point I have even participated in lengthy testing meetings where I've done about forty or fifty hits of various strains, then gone straight into an afternoon conference call without noticeable impairment.

This is actually consistent with the science on marijuana. Studies do show that people react differently to marijuana and that people do build up a tolerance to the drug over time with frequent use. In some studies, however, the tolerance has been shown to be *nonuniform.*

That means that while one hit of a joint no longer gives long-time users the same high and their cognitive function remains unimpaired, the bud will still impact them physically. They don't get as high, but the product still eradicates their aches and pains. In general, this tends to be good news for a lot of our medical patients. They don't need to smoke more to feel better physically.

Perhaps my tolerance has something to do with my size or my general metabolism, but it's always been that way, even when I was an adolescent. My brother and his friends would be stoned on one or two hits, but I'd need ten to reach that point. Once, when I got into the business, I happened to share a joint with a friend. One puff affected him so strongly that I needed to stub out the joint and take him out for lunch and a beer—anything to process that THC out of his system.

Only a few of my employees allow themselves to smoke when we're in these meetings. They know that they're better off getting high on their own time. As fun a place as ours is to work, it's still work. They don't want to be laughing giddily when we need them to think cogently. A few hits will throw them off their game for the rest of the meeting, or even the afternoon. So most don't indulge.

But those of us with a high tolerance—me, Corey, and Barb—*will* light up, smoke, and discuss the finer points of the product.

So this is Grape Cola. Cool.

I see the purple color and I'm getting the astringent smell I'd expect from the bud. Nice.

It tastes good and the effect is nicely indica, but not too overbearing.

Oh, this is Sour Diesel.

Yeah—but the diesel smell is off. It won't sell.

People will call bullshit if we try to pass this off as Sour D, even though the provenance and taste are there. Without that smell it won't sell.

We were excited. The Cannabis Cup was coming to Denver for the second time in history. *High Times,* the same magazine I'd read as a kid when I was first initiated into the mysteries of cannabis, has sponsored a legendary Amsterdam event each November for the past thirty years. In 2010, *High Times* began running events in the U.S. states where marijuana was legal. As I write this, the magazine now runs six events worldwide every year—in Seattle; Los Angeles; San Francisco; Denver; Clio, Michigan; and Amsterdam, of course.

It was time for another strain selection party. We were going for the big one.

THE NUMBER 420 holds a special significance for marijuana enthusiasts. The trouble is, no one has bothered to record precisely why the number is special. I've heard various theories. One legend says it's the time—4:20 p.m.—when a group of weed-smoking teenagers would gather outside their high school in San Rafael, California, in the 1970s to light up. Others say that the 420 tradition originated in a 1939 short story by the science fiction writer H. P. Lovecraft, in which an explorer to the planet Venus falls under the influence of a mysterious, hallucinogenic "mirage-plant" that sounds a lot like marijuana. When the explorer's reverie ceases, the man looks at his watch and is "astonished to find the time was only 4:20."

Regardless of the origin, this number has inspired millions of people worldwide to designate April 20 as the day marijuana smokers raise a silent joint in honor of their blessed herb.

Well, on that day in April 2012, Denver's EXDO Center, a city block with outdoor space connecting four separate buildings, was packed to the gills with thirty thousand people. A sell-out crowd. For three days I had been hawking our wares out of a booth.

The Cannabis Cup looked like every trade show you've ever attended—with one exception. Everything you saw was devoted to the glory of marijuana.

You know those trade shows where people give you key chains and candy and other useless trinkets? Imagine instead walking down the aisle and being invited to take a hit from a bong or vaporizer.

You can't pull off a show like this easily. For one thing, since transporting marijuana across state lines is still a violation of federal law, the state of Colorado had officials on site to check that every ounce of marijuana was sourced from a Colorado grower. In that respect, it was a little like a dog or antiques show. Every ounce had its own papers, its own provenance.

You had to be eighteen to get in the doors and have a valid red card to be able to enter the designated "medicating"—that is, *smoking* area, which you could easily spot as soon as you entered. It was where everyone was headed: the building in the EXDO Center that was filled with a thick, resinous cloud. Our booth was located there.

I had taken our precious Colorado Cup off the shelf and transported it to a place of honor in the center of our booth. It was bolted down to the table with a high-tech cable, and our staffers took turns lighting it all weekend long.

People were loving it.

Every day I was on my feet for eight hours, passing out brochures, selling our Green Man T-shirts, and inviting people to try out our products.

I was baked off my ass.

Seriously, I've never been so high in my entire life. At one point I thought I was hallucinating.

Forget what I just said about my legendary tolerance. Tolerance meets its match in a 20,000-square-foot hall packed with a steady stream of people and clouds of marijuana smoke. People came in, took their hits, exhaled, then walked out of our booth, only to be replaced by others who did exactly the same thing. Eventually the cloud of smoke inside this large exhibit hall was dense. Simply breathing in this space was like taking a little hit with every breath.

My head was swimming. It was actually stimulating to be in the presence of so many people who no longer had to hide the fact that they enjoyed marijuana.

The other buildings and the outdoor area of the EXDO Center were smoke-free. There the show featured a good number of educational sessions throughout the weekend. People were learning how to set up their own grows. Fitness instructors we giving classes on how to exercise and manage pain with marijuana. Activist attorneys were lecturing on various aspects of the legalization movement. There were panel discussions on how our society would be changed by the presence of legal marijuana.

Most people were there to smoke and shop and enjoy the music. To take it all in, to be part of this moment of change. Images of the marijuana leaf were everywhere. The rediscovery of marijuana in modern America owes a lot to young hippies who embraced the drug in the 1960s. Remarkably, much of what I was seeing that weekend was merely an extension of the old 1960s imagery.

It made me wonder: If marijuana was going to grow beyond the demographic of enthusiasts, would it need to adopt a new imagery or look?

I wanted our business to grow. Everyone was talking about the possibility that marijuana would one day be legal for all adults in the state of Colorado, not just those with medical conditions. If adult recreational use was approved, we'd see a new clientele in our dispensaries. People who had always been curious about smoking marijuana but were not willing to break the law to try it. People who had sneaked a smoke as adolescents but who never smoked it again as adults.

If you wanted those people to feel comfortable giving you their business, was the tie-dyed aesthetic of the 1960s still the way to go? Or did we need a new aesthetic?

I knew I was on to something, but I was too busy to give it more than a fleeting thought. But that show was what got me thinking about the ways in which branding permeates our lives.

I'd venture to say that anyone in the world who sees a distinctive red-and-white swirl on any product will immediately think "Coca-Cola," even though those words or their abbreviation, "Coke," is nowhere to be found on the object. Show anyone a swoosh design on sporting apparel and they will immediately know the brand even if the critical four letters—N-I-K-E—are not present. The same goes for that little transparent apple with the bite taken out of it; millions know what that symbol stands for.

Admittedly, I've chosen three of the world's biggest brands. But lesser brands are still highly recognizable by their logos, and that recognizability can have an enormous impact on those brands' fortunes. Chances are good, for example, that you have at some point in your life seen someone wearing a T-shirt or sweatshirt with the image of a black dog on it. Those shirts are the brand of the Black

Dog Tavern, which opened in 1971 on Martha's Vineyard in Massachusetts. Today the brand has grown to include numerous gift shops and general stores. When you see someone wearing one of those shirts, your recognition of that brand is reinforced. Should your travels take you to Massachusetts, you're likely to make a point of visiting one of the company's locations—if only to see what all the fuss is about.

Our industry was still small, so small that a Black Dog, a Sam Adams, an Apple, or a Starbucks had yet to emerge. But in time, one certainly would.

For now, our T-shirts featured the face of the Green Man—a spirit of nature from ancient pagan lore. High as I was, as I stood there in the hall watching cannabis fans get higher still around me, I thought it was a question worth pondering: Was it possible to make my brand as recognizable as that black dog or that swoosh or that smiling Boston patriot brandishing a tankard of beer?

I didn't know it then, but I was about to be handed one tool to hasten that brand recognition. Our first order of business, even before setting up our booth, was to drop off our 40-gram samples for the cannabis competition. Over the course of ten days, the judges would be smoking the entrants' weed, and the winners would be announced on the last night of the show.

We didn't overthink our entry that year. We were justifiably proud of our SkunkBerry strain because we were the first company to produce it commercially. Brandon, my second grower, introduced us to it, and the strain was flourishing in Corey's care.

It's an interesting little bud. SkunkBerry has a very potent odor of skunk, which is mellowed by a very real fragrance of blueberry pie. The two flavors temper each other. The skunk never gets angry; it's just tangy. The blueberry is sweet, not cloying. And in the background, if you wait for it, you'll detect a pleasing sharp, astringent odor that also comes through in the taste of the smoke. It is very distinctive.

This strain does well in our shops, but we didn't really know how the judges would take to it. When you're smoking SkunkBerry, you know it. There's nothing subtle about it. The flavors are so clearly different from what you just smoked or are about to smoke. Would the judges enjoy that palate shift, or not?

Come Sunday, the exhibitors closed up shop and cleared the floor. Attendees packed in to hear the announcements. Typically, the smaller awards are read off first, but today, for some reason, the judges started at the top and worked their way down.

Corey had convinced me that his "lucky spot" was standing in the back of the room. So we had all congregated together far from the stage. Just as things got started, I heard the judges say, "Green Man Cannabis!"

"Hey, they called out our name!" I said to one of my employees. "What was that for?"

"I think it was for the Cannabis Cup for Hybrid!"

This is the highest award in the industry, given for general excellence. The Best Picture Oscar for Marijuana, you might say. Because our industry is small, those who win the Cannabis Cup are roundly accorded bragging rights for the rest of their lives.

I didn't think it was probable.

"No," I told the employee. "It can't be. They must be starting from the third prize and working their way up."

"No, you won!" someone said. "Go! Go get your prize!"

I felt the shove of a half dozen hands, pushing me toward the stage.

We were so far in the back of the room that the judges had assumed we were no longer present. Someone else had leaped forward to accept the prize on my behalf. But then, just as he was walking away, I popped up on stage followed by my partners and employees.

"Oh, wait," someone said. "Green Man is here."

I was stunned. My hands were trembling, I couldn't believe what had just happened. I'd started this business three years ago, and now our company and its employees had taken an award known through-out the world for cannabis excellence.

Tell me: In what other industry in corporate America could a young company achieve such an award in so short a time?

I was so grateful. I could not have done it without our team, especially our grower Corey. He now had three Cannabis Cup wins under his belt.

The actual cup is an underwhelming trophy. An acquaintance of mine once showed me the trophy he had won for mixed doubles at Wimbledon, and I was surprised how small it was. I suppose I had expected something along the lines of the 25-pound Heisman Trophy. The Cannabis Cup was nothing like that: it was only 7 inches tall from its base to the top of the cup, and the caduceus—the snakes-and-staff symbol that signifies the medical field—served as the stem, morphing into two iconic-looking marijuana leaves that held up a golden bowl.

I took the cup and waved it over my head.

The audience went wild.

11

MARIJUANA'S MECCA

IN THE WORLD OF CANNABIS, THERE IS ONE NAME THAT
stands out when you begin talking about growing marijuana: Ed
Rosenthal. The *New York Times* once described him as "the pothead's answer to Ann Landers, Judge Judy, Martha Stewart and the
Burpee Garden Wizard all in one." The latest edition of Ed's book is
dedicated to Pete Seeger. The foreword is written by Tommy Chong,
the activist and actor of Cheech and Chong fame.

Though he's not formally trained as a horticulturist, Ed traveled
the world studying marijuana cultivation, back when it was still illegal and unpopular to do so in the United States. He churned out
a number of books that patiently taught two generations of underground growers how it's done. If you ask professional growers today
what reference book they recommend you read before setting up a
grow, they will all recommend *Ed Rosenthal's Marijuana Grower's
Handbook.*

In October 2011, the autumn before our 2012 Cannabis Cup
win, I got a call one afternoon from Dr. Paul Bregman, a former ra-
diologist in Denver who is now a major figure in the cannabis movement and has testified as an expert witness before the state legislature
on medical marijuana issues. Paul said that Ed Rosenthal was visiting

Colorado. He was in Denver *that night.* Did I have time to join a group of them for dinner with Ed?

At first I thought it was one of these events where fifty people sat in an audience while Ed spoke. That type of thing didn't interest me. But Paul insisted this would be different. He had scored Ed's phone number and called him a few days ago. Ed had agreed to meet Paul for dinner one night while in Denver; he didn't have other plans. It was to be only four or five people, plus Ed. I couldn't pass up the opportunity.

"Hell, yeah," I told Paul on the phone. "I'll see you there."

We were all meeting at the Imperial Chinese restaurant on Broadway. I went—but not before visiting our dispensary and picking up some choice buds of a strain known as the Ed Rosenthal Super Bud. It's a fascinating hybrid of both sativa and indica that results in freakishly huge buds. Some people say it has a flavor profile not unlike pineapple punch; others describe it as having a citrusy, earthy, minty flavor.

The fact that we could even talk about these flavors was due to the man I was about to meet. Among other things, Ed had made a careful study of terpenes, the aromatic essential oils that were found in cannabis resin and that gave all plants—not just marijuana—their powerful scents. When I read Ed's books, I was reminded again of Nature's resourcefulness. When Nature found a scent that worked well—the smell of lemons, for example—she didn't just put them in lemons. Nature injects that odor in the form of limonene in herbs such as lemon balm and marijuana plants. This antibacterial, antifungal, and anticancer terpene protects those plants from predators. As Ed has pointed out in his books over the years, the reason Nature endowed cannabis with THC-secreting glands is to help the plant ward off animals that would be moved to eat it. But ingeniously, that very same defense mechanism helped the plant attract the only animals that could ensure the plant's success throughout the world: human beings.

I got to the restaurant. Everyone was still standing, shaking hands with this gnomelike fellow with outrageously unkempt hair. He was small, thin, and somewhere in his sixties.

Out came the soup.

As the waiters were doing their thing, I pulled the bag from my pocket and quietly announced that I had brought some Ed Rosenthal Super Bud for Ed to check out. I handed the bag to the guy on my right, who lovingly inspected it before passing it down the table to the next guy, and the next, until it finally reached Ed.

The conversation at the table turned briefly to how Super Bud came to be named after Ed. The owner of Sensi Seed, a good friend of Ed's, had named two strains in honor of two men who had done so much for marijuana—one strain after the late activist Jack Herer and another strain after Ed. I could tell Ed was not overly excited to be presented with his own bud, but he was pleased to be recognized and liked that our bud was really well grown.

The night wore on. At the end of our dinner, Ed pulled me aside. He looked at the bag of Super Bud. "Thank you so much for showing these to me. They're beautiful. So . . . do you want to go smoke them?"

You can guess what my answer was. When you have the opportunity to smoke weed with one of the great figures of the industry—and that opportunity involves smoking a strain named after him—the answer is not yes but *"Hell, yes!"*

Ed and I and all the others from dinner went out to where I'd parked my Chevy Tahoe and climbed inside. I packed a bowl in a glass pipe, which I had brought just in case, and offered it up to Ed. After one puff, Ed started talking about the qualities of the bud in that bowl with the discernment of a true connoisseur. His description of the look, smell, taste, and high was so specific, so on the nose, that I knew I was in the presence of a master and still had much to learn.

I can't believe this, I thought. I'm smoking Ed Rosenthal Super Bud in my car with Ed Rosenthal himself.

We got to talking. Ed struck me as intensely knowledgeable. You couldn't just ask him a question about marijuana and expect to get a quick yes-or-no answer. "Yes," he would say, "but there are four parts to that answer. Do you want to hear them all?"

Before the night was over, I asked him if he'd like to come by and check out our grows. He said he'd be happy to. He just needed to check his schedule. Okay, I thought, that's his way of letting me down. He's busy seeing a lot of other people in Colorado while he's here.

But sure enough, the next day, Ed showed up, eager to check out what we'd been up to. All the growers who worked for me were astonished and perhaps a little bit nervous. "Oh, Mr. Rosenthal," they would say as they came up to him, "I have your book!"

After that, Ed and I became friends and started working on a business opportunity together. One that involved me going to Amsterdam with him at some point to meet some people who needed to find a business home in the United States.

Well, the night we won the Cannabis Cup, Ed was there. And he was one of the first to throw his arms around me and give me a huge hug of congratulations.

"It's time we go to Amsterdam," he said. "You ready for this?" Considering I'd spent two exhausting days exhibiting at the Cannabis Cup and was still high from winning the top award, it was a reasonable question.

I had never been to Amsterdam. I'm pretty well traveled, but I somehow missed the college marijuana excursion to Amsterdam, where you got to pose as a world traveler when really all you did in Europe was get baked in a marijuana café. Ed and I had talked previously about what we would need to accomplish while there. I knew I would be meeting a lot of people who had worked in the Dutch marijuana industry for decades. I was going to Mount Olympus to meet the Gods of Weed.

I told myself it was a smart thing to do for the business. We weren't just a bunch of start-up newbies anymore. We had won the Cannabis Cup, for heaven's sake. Ed and I had booked the trip earlier, so my calendar was clear. I packed my bags, bade my wife and daughters good-bye, and headed to Amsterdam in the company of the biggest name in weed. Our Cannabis Cup win was only forty-eight hours old by the time we touched down in the great city of the Dutch.

Amsterdam lived up to its reputation as a beautiful, progressive city. On our first day, Ed wanted to initiate me by taking me to one of the city's best marijuana cafés. He rushed along the sidewalk, traipsing past the canals and bridges that define Amsterdam, passing one café after another. We were not far from the famous Herengracht, the historic "Gentleman's Canal," where Amsterdam's elite had lived in centuries past. I tagged along after him, peering into the windows of one inviting café after another. I saw bars and comfortable seats and fetching artwork on the walls.

"What about this one?" I said. "Or this one? Or this one?"

"No," he snapped without turning around. "It's not the best. I know it's right up here somewhere."

I don't know, I thought. The ones we're passing look pretty nice to me.

And of course, when he finally spotted the café he was looking for, it was a closet with a window. We crammed ourselves inside the legendary Grey Area, its walls covered with bumper stickers and decals in tons of different languages. There were only a few tables, and people were known to sit, half in, half out, in the café's front windows. The clerk presented us with a couple of menus. One listed soft drinks. The other was divided into WEED and HASH options. Incredible.

While we studied our choices, the clerk stared at Ed for a while, then stepped away. When he came back, Ed gave him our order. The café offered a range of rolling papers so we could roll our own and smoke right at the bar.

You don't just read a menu when you're with Ed. Reviewing the list of options sparked a monologue. He held forth on each of the strains, spelling out for me who had bred each, when it was first presented to the public, what awards each had won, and which other strains used this particular one as a successful breeding pair.

"How much do we owe you?" Ed said offhandedly to the clerk.

"Nothing, Mr. Rosenthal," the clerk said. "We're very happy to see you again."

"Thank you, it's nice to be back." Ed said.

"I can't charge you," the clerk said. "I just phoned the owner that you were here in person, and those are his instructions. He's coming over right now to meet you."

We would get the same reaction everywhere else we went. Everyone seemed to recognize Ed. Ed explained that some years ago, he had become one of the most visible faces in the Netherlands during a court case regarding marijuana. That, and the fact that his cultivation handbooks had sold more than a million copies worldwide, ensured that he was likely to be recognized anywhere he went in the kingdom of marijuana.

I can't tell you how many of those cafés we visited that week. At a certain point they all melded into a wondrous blur. I was falling in love with the city. It was liberating to be able to sit in a café and watch people come in, sip a bottle of mineral water or an espresso coffee, all the while enjoying a joint or a bowl from a glass pipe, then get up and go on their merry way. There was no shame to it. It seemed sophisticated, urbane, and freeing.

Sometimes Ed would introduce me as the recent American winner of the Cannabis Cup, a fact that engendered a lot of curiosity from Amsterdammers and others. They were fascinated at the notion that cannabis was slowly becoming legal in America, and they had lots of questions. I was beginning to realize that, even in such a progressive place as Amsterdam, what was happening in the United States was nothing short of revolutionary.

It is not obvious to tourists, but cannabis laws in the Netherlands are quite strict. You could still get busted if you smoked weed or hash outdoors in public, beyond the safety of a private café. It is still illegal to grow cannabis in the Netherlands. Growers were routinely busted when discovered. Cafés, I was told, were permitted to keep only 100 grams—a mere 3.5 ounces—on the premises at any given time. By contrast, my Colorado dispensaries routinely kept 20 *pounds* of buds on site at all times to meet demand. Amsterdam's strict regulations begged the question: How did all these marijuana cafés keep from running out?

One day I learned the truth. As soon as a café depleted its stock, a courier on a bicycle mysteriously appeared at the door with a fresh, 100-gram infusion of weed and hash. I assumed someone in the café had made a surreptitious phone call, but it happened so seamlessly that if you didn't know to watch for it, you'd never notice it at all.

One day as we wound our way through Ed's whirlwind cannabis tour, we encountered a thin man whose dreadlocks seemed to run all the way down to the ground. He stopped short and greeted Ed warmly. They chatted briefly before Ed introduced us.

"Chris, this is Soma."

No fucking way, I thought.

Soma was the founder of Soma Seeds, which sold cannabis seeds to growers all over the world. Soma's past is somewhat shrouded in mystery. On his website he tells how he first smoked marijuana back in 1967, when he was working as a mail clerk at an IBM office in New York City. Back then, he was a straight shooter who went off to work each morning clad in a three-piece suit and tie. But the first puff of marijuana changed his life. He ended up devoting his life to marijuana when it was still illegal throughout the United States. At one point he was growing in Vermont, presumably trying to stay one step ahead of the law. By the time he fled to Amsterdam and started going by the name Soma, he had come to regard marijuana as a sacred, versatile plant. He wore clothes fashioned of hemp and smoked regularly. Today, like Ed, he is another international legend in the world of cannabis.

He invited Ed and me to visit with him at his apartment, and a short time later we found ourselves in the most bohemian flat I had ever seen in my entire life. Those tall windows that grace so many of Amsterdam's historic buildings imbued the living room with sunlight. I learned that every time friends visited Soma, they brought him rocks from their homeland. The floor was covered with rocks of every type of size, color, and origin. Interspersed among them were bright pillows. That's how he entertained us: We sat on the floor amid the pillows and rocks, smoked our weed, and talked about our common business.

I suppose if anyone had seen us, they would have been struck by the juxtaposition of a best-selling author, a dreadlocked outlaw, and an American businessman enjoying each other's company. Ed and Soma were undoubtedly the more courageous; they had taken risks that had made their lives difficult over the years, all in service to the herb.

In 2002, Ed had been arrested by federal agents when he was found to be managing a marijuana nursery in Oakland, California. The feds threatened him with twenty years in prison, but Ed refused to take a plea. The way he saw it, he was in the right and the feds were wrong. First, he had been growing those plants with the blessing of Oakland's municipal administration and its city attorney. The plants in that nursery were earmarked as starter plants for the city's medical marijuana patients. (Medical marijuana has been legal in California since 1996.) Ed had been working on behalf of his local government, and now he was on the hook for felony charges and looking at a long prison sentence. He and an attorney from the National Organization for the Reform of Marijuana Laws (NORML) fought the charges in court. The judge ultimately took Ed's side, sentencing him to time served plus one day in jail. I could not help thinking how coura-geously Ed had faced that nightmare. Most people would have been afraid to take the case to court. They would have allowed the fed-eral government to intimidate them; they would have taken the plea agreement and done the time.

Each of us—Soma, Ed, and I—had approached marijuana in our own way. I was thrilled to be in the presence of these pioneers. It was one of the most enlightening times I've spent in this industry. Without their sacrifices over the years, I would not have been able to pursue the business I was in.

One day Ed took me to one of the Green House Seeds cafés in Amsterdam. The café was large and nicely appointed. When we ar-rived, Soma was sitting at the bud bar, smoking away. Turned out he was dating the budtender, a beautiful, much-younger woman who had been at his flat the other day. While sitting there smoking with Ed and Soma again, I saw displayed on the far wall not one but *twen-ty-one* Cannabis Cups. (The firm has won more than thirty-five Can-nabis Cups for strain excellence under the tutelage of Arjan Roskam, who is known as the king of cannabis.) I was blown away. Humbled, actually. Wow, I thought, I've got a lot of catching up to do.

You cannot think of Amsterdam without thinking of those pretty canals and small boats and cyclists everywhere. Every home appears to have been built at a time when aesthetics still mattered. Every ca-nal you see has been dug by human hands, so the Dutch could float their goods and possessions gracefully down waterways instead of hauling them overland. I admired the sorts of minds who could build a city with such intention. The Dutch didn't seem to sweat the small stuff. The whole nation, so far as I could see, got around on beat-up bicycles. If one was swiped from its stand, I couldn't see them fretting about it. They probably just went out and bought another beat-up bi-cycle. One night, while Ed and I were smoking in a café, I happened to look out the window to see a family of three—father, mother, and daughter, all tall, all blond—pushing their bicycles home with their groceries tucked in their baskets. Their calm, accepting expressions as they passed a busy marijuana café spoke volumes to me.

In Ed's company I would later stroll along those canals, drinking in the city's relaxed atmosphere and hitting every marijuana establishment we could, and a few museums too. The owner of Sensi Seeds, Ben Dronkers, also owns the world-famous Hash Marihuana & Hemp Museum. We were guests of Ben's and were staying in his apartment directly above this museum. One of the reasons Ed had come to Amsterdam this specific week was to attend to the Cannabis Culture Awards, and he brought me along with him.

That event was an eye-opening experience for this naive if otherwise worldly American. Here I was with people like the billionaire founder of the Virgin Group, Sir Richard Branson, who had served on the United Nations' global commission on drug policy, which was calling on world nations to institute sensible drug policies and admit that the decades-long "drug war" had not worked. The commission on which Branson had served was receiving the Cannabis Culture Award from the museum for its work. The former foreign minister of Norway, Thorvald Stoltenberg, was accepting the award on the commission's behalf. That award was being presented by Dries van Agt, the former president of the Netherlands.

Titans of industry and heads of state hobnobbing together, happily gathering to accept an award from a *marijuana* museum? In what kind of bizarro universe had I just landed?

What was happening around me forced me to rethink the culture I had left behind in the United States.

On one hand, the laws governing legal marijuana in Colorado and California were far less restrictive that what was going on in the Netherlands. But for the life of me, I could not imagine going to a marijuana award event in the United States and discovering, say, Microsoft's Bill Gates, former president Bill Clinton, and both of the former presidents Bush in attendance.

Imagine that they had all served on a committee that found marijuana drug policy to be a waste of time, money, and effort. Imagine if they were telling world nations to relax their policies on this plant because the evidence showed it to be relatively benign compared to, say, alcohol and tobacco.

Sadly, I could not imagine such a thing happening. Not for a long, long time.

I left the event that night having two powerful feelings.

One: What the hell am I doing here among these people? Three years ago, I wasn't even in this business, and now I'm sitting with presidents and foreign ministers of various countries, talking about weed!

Two: How bad can marijuana be if these corporate presidents and foreign politicians see value in easing up laws restricting it?

I've always been an early riser. Each morning, I'd leave our flat above the museum early and walk the streets of Amsterdam well before people were heading off to work. It struck me that Amsterdam is a little like Europe's Vegas. When young men from the UK want to celebrate a buddy's bachelor party, they head to 'Dam, and spend a couple of nights making fools of themselves amid the hookers and clubs and marijuana cafés.

But now, as I watched in the early morning hours, I was amazed to see the waves of street cleaners go about their business, carefully erasing all evidence of the previous night's debauchery from Amsterdam's streets. By the time I was thinking of grabbing a newspaper and my morning coffee, last night's puke, trash, and broken bottles had disappeared. The city of canals had been transformed into a pristine city once again.

What did that say about the Dutch, I wondered, that they were so comfortable having both sides of human nature—debauchery and civility—dwell so intimately beside each other without getting bent out of shape about it?

HIGH **HAS TO BE ONE** of the most overused words in my profession, but I assure you that when I returned home from my trip, I was brimming with a natural sort of elation. The Amsterdam trip had opened my eyes. I had seen how other cultures embraced our little plant. I had bonded with one of world's top cannabis experts, whom I now counted as a friend. And I had seen how our Cannabis Cup win back home could open doors abroad.

No doubt about it—I was a happy SOB.

Soon after I got home, I took a trip out of town with my wife. While we were away, I got an anxious call from my grow team. At the time, we were still mired in our legal issues with two of our dispensary partners. An emergency appeal had been filed with Colorado's Medical Marijuana Enforcement Division, seeking to sever our relationship.

Once that emergency severance went into effect, we could not lawfully continue to grow all the plants covered by our partnerships. Three enforcement officers from the Department of Revenue had shown up at our grow and rounded up all the plants that had been tagged and earmarked for those two dispensaries. The officers used shrub clippers to hack all the plants from their growing mediums. They bundled up all the butchered plants—nearly half of our stock—stuffed them in giant plastic bags, and whisked them away.

As soon as I got back to town, I rushed down to the offices of the MMED to find out what I could. The officer I met with welcomed me into his office and told me to take a seat. "Hey," he said with an awkward grin on his face. "I just came from burning your plants."

They had rented an incinerator from the DEA not far from the airport to do the deed.

I felt sucker-punched. Those plants represented about $100,000. I took it well, I thought. I reminded myself that I could have failures but still not fail. The Cannabis Cup win was a good barometer of our place in the business. Still . . . $100,000 lost? That was a big loss to come back from.

My award-winning plants had just gone up in smoke. I had gone from so high to so low so quickly.

12

MARIJUANA ON
THE BALLOT

THE CLOCK WAS TICKING.

I pulled my iPhone out of my pocket and checked the front page of the *Denver Post*.

My eyes flicked down the headlines.

Nothing yet.

I stuck the phone back into my pocket and tried to get on with my day. But it was a little tough. I had a meeting that morning, and right after, as soon as I got back to my office, I pulled up the browser on my computer screen to check the news again.

The fate of my business—and so many others—rested with three counties in the state.

Still nothing.

It was Election Day, November 2012.

The citizens of our state had a big decision to make today, well beyond the battle for the presidency between the incumbent, President Obama, and the former governor of Massachusetts, Mitt Romney. No, every marijuana activist and enthusiast in the country was dying to know which way voters would swing on the matter of Colorado Amendment 64. Would they approve it or give it a pass?

Until now, marijuana sales in the state had been restricted to medical use only. Anyone who wanted to buy had to jump through the same hoops I had when I'd first gotten my medical red card years ago. But the question before the voters today was whether to permit the sale of marijuana *to adults age twenty-one or older for adult recreational use.* The precise wording of the referendum went like this:

> Shall there be an amendment to the Colorado constitution concerning marijuana, and, in connection therewith, providing for the regulation of marijuana; permitting a person twenty-one years of age or older to consume or possess limited amounts of marijuana; providing for the licensing of cultivation facilities, product manufacturing facilities, testing facilities, and retail stores; permitting local governments to regulate or prohibit such facilities; requiring the general assembly to enact an excise tax to be levied upon wholesale sales of marijuana; requiring that the first $40 million in revenue raised annually by such tax be credited to the public school capital construction assistance fund; and requiring the general assembly to enact legislation governing the cultivation, processing, and sale of industrial hemp?

To my mind, the clunky legislative wording shook down to a couple of critical yes/no questions:

- Should law-abiding grown-ups be allowed to buy marijuana the way they bought cigarettes and tobacco—yes or no?
- Should those law-abiding grown-ups be allowed to grow up to six plants of marijuana in their homes, within reasonable restrictions—yes or no?
- Should they be able to possess or give as a gift to some other adult up to 1 ounce of marijuana without penalty—yes or no?

- Should dispensaries like mine be allowed to sell up to 1 ounce at a time to any adult age twenty-one or older—yes or no?

How the voters decided would have a huge impact on the way we did business. Such a law, if approved, could theoretically propel our sales into the stratosphere. It would transform the way citizens of the United States and the world viewed Colorado. In the same way that college kids dreamed of going to Amsterdam to drink in that city's marijuana-friendly lifestyle, they would now dream of vacations to Colorado for reasons well beyond the state's legendary ski slopes and mountain peaks.

We in the business were excited about the possibilities. In the past few years, I'd come to know so many different types of people who I saw as potential customers. There were high-functioning, otherwise law-abiding people who nevertheless smoked weed on a daily basis. Some continued to obtain their product the way they always had—illegally on the street. They didn't like doing so, but they had made their peace with this compromise a long time ago.

Others had been emboldened enough to apply for red cards. They had legitimate reasons for doing so, but they didn't want this part of their lives to become public knowledge. There was still too much of a stigma attached to marijuana. They didn't want their friends and neighbors to think they had exploited a loophole in the law just to get high.

And there were still others I met regularly who were curious about the herb but had never indulged for a very good reason: They feared breaking the law.

Until marijuana came out of the closet and was regarded by our culture as similar to a glass of wine at the end of day, each of these different classes of people would not rest easy.

The ballot initiative had been approved back in February 2012, and since then, a spirited debate had flourished in the media.

Surprisingly, quite a few of my colleagues in the industry thought that all-out legalization was the wrong way to go. They professed a fear of Amendment 64, and their objections seemed to be tainted with the old paranoia. They worried that if the amendment passed, the feds would grow impatient with Colorado's newfound permissiveness and crack down in the form of new legislation and enforcement. "Don't you see?" these people reasoned. "We have a good thing going with medical marijuana. If you really want it, you can apply for it and get it. Why do we have to rock the boat?"

I had a unique perspective on the battle for legalization. One of our attorneys, Christian Sederberg, and his partner Brian Vicente were instrumental in writing various state initiatives over the years, not just for Colorado but for other states, calling for more humane, realistic, and mature drug policies. They and activists from advocacy groups such as the Marijuana Policy Project, SAFER (Safer Alternative For Enjoyable Recreation), and the Colorado chapter of NORML had lobbied for years to make marijuana legal in our state, but their message had never clicked with the mainstream public. Interestingly, all these groups recently moved into the same building near the state capital building in Denver. Those of us in the business call it the Marijuana Mansion. It is the epicenter of thought leadership for the growing national marijuana industry.

Leading up to this Election Day, these groups tried a new approach. In their polling, they realized that many voters were still laboring under the delusion that marijuana was just another vice that was likely to be abused like alcohol. In the absence of solid information on the matter, the average citizen was assuming that marijuana was more harmful than booze. So why would they vote to add yet another way for people to destroy the lives of themselves and others?

That was the sticking point. These citizens had marijuana all wrong.

In 2012, the activists worked hard to get one important message across to voters: *Marijuana was safer than alcohol.*

Period.

The evidence for their claim was statistically and evidentially valid. Every year, alcohol caused the deaths of 35,000 people in the United States. Alcohol was an addictive substance. Even those who were not alcoholics stood a chance of overdosing on alcohol. When drunk, citizens often abused their loved ones and others. A drunk behind the wheel of a car was a disaster in the making. You didn't have to persuade people of these facts. All Americans know this in their bones.

In contrast, it was virtually impossible to overdose on marijuana. As far back as 1937, when the federal government made the substance illegal, experts had found it to be nonaddictive. And the statistics just weren't there to support the notion that people who were high on marijuana abused or killed others. Hell, you could get high on Sunday night and not even suffer a hangover come Monday. There was a good argument to be made that if the substance was legal, more people would avail themselves of the safer alternative; they'd get high, chill out, laugh a lot, scarf down a pizza, and stay safe indoors instead of getting drunk and risk hurting themselves or others.

All year long, ad campaigns had driven home this one simple message. Polling indicated that more and more people in the state were receptive to this thinking. The numbers were in favor of legalization, but they were still close enough to make those of us in the industry nervous. A few conservative counties in the state presented a significant hurdle to passage. I knew a lot of people who thought the same way as these county residents did. After a lifetime of hearing negative press on marijuana, would they really be willing to change their opinions? Would they buy the argument or assume it was a lie?

As a father, I was not unsympathetic to the notion that legal marijuana would present some challenges to all of us, but I thought the good outweighed the bad. If marijuana was legal, my children would someday be likely to try it. Perhaps they would even procure fake IDs the way young people did to buy alcohol. But at least there would be a budtender on the other side of the counter inspecting their IDs. Last time I checked, drug dealers don't card. Drug dealers also don't offer a legitimate, clean, seed-to-sale provenance for their product. There literally is no telling where the weed you bought off the street came from, or what it was adulterated with. In some instances, drug dealers are also selling cocaine, meth, and other illegal drugs right alongside their illegal marijuana.

Legal marijuana would open a can of worms for the state's police officers. When someone's been drinking, you can test their blood alcohol content with a Breathalyzer test. The level of THC in one's blood can be determined only by a blood draw or urine sample. (At this writing, Colorado and Washington both use a 5-nanogram-per-milliliter driving-under-the-influence-of-drugs standard.) That means that a suspected driver would need to be taken into custody and escorted to a police station or hospital so the test can be administered. That test would need to be conducted soon after the road stop, and the suspect would need to be accompanied by a police officer the whole time to ensure the chain of evidence. That is a problem. One suspected stoner driving under the influence could effectively put one police officer out of rotation for an entire shift. That manpower sacrifice could be problematic for most police departments. To make matters worse, law enforcement agencies, marijuana activists, and researchers are still debating whether the 5-nanogram standard is reasonable. Some think it's too low; others insist it's too high.

I am not arguing that these issues don't present significant challenges. But if marijuana was legal, police officers would no longer be charged with busting people for possession. The entire judicial system would see a radical decrease in drug cases. This seems like a more than worthwhile trade-off.

I also saw a benefit for my medical marijuana clientele. Many of the people I saw in our dispensaries truly were sick. Their daily schedules consisted of going from one doctor's appointment to another. Under the current system, medical marijuana red cards had to be renewed each year. If marijuana was legal for all adults, these sick patients wouldn't have to jump through hoops every year to get certified. They could just walk into a dispensary anytime they wanted, no questions asked.

The day of the vote, Ed Rosenthal was in town, and we spent some time together, talking about the significance of the referendum. Later in the afternoon I was tied up with a few administrative issues and took some phone calls. I didn't know what had happened until I heard some employees cheering.

I went out of my office and saw a group of people gathered around a computer. It was still early in the afternoon. The polls had not yet closed. We were still a long way from knowing who had won the presidency, but the votes were in on marijuana. The three critical counties had swung in favor of YES to Amendment 64.

Later that night, the story got even better. Obama had taken all nine of Colorado's electoral votes. But the number of Coloradans who had voted for him (51 percent) was still fewer than the number of people (53 percent) who voted for marijuana.

Weed was more popular than the president.

Up in Washington state, voters had passed Initiative Measure 502, legalizing marijuana in their state, by a margin of 56 percent to 44 percent.

It was a fascinating election night. Voters in two U.S. states had said yes to marijuana. Our governor took to the airwaves that night, announcing that the state would live up to the letter of the law. "But don't break out the Cheetos and Goldfish too quickly," he quipped.

On that Tuesday evening in November, all of our facilities were fully staffed. We didn't exactly follow the governor's advice. In our elation, we rolled some joints and walked proudly outside each building. On the chilly streets of Denver, we lit up and puffed away to celebrate the birth of a new market and the turning of the tide.

WHAT WAS THE RESULT of that momentous night?

The law didn't go into effect until New Year's Day 2014, a Wednesday. In Denver, people started lining up outside their nearest dispensaries on New Year's Eve, braving the chilly Colorado weather in their sweaters, parkas, and scarves to be first in line to buy the next morning.

The law was clear. Locals could buy up to 1 ounce at a time, visitors a quarter of an ounce. You couldn't smoke in public, and you could not hoard your stash by buying, say, 1 ounce a day until you had enough marijuana in your mattress to choke Tommy Chong. Anyone found with more than 8 ounces in their possession would be looking at felony charges. The most prudent course of action was to buy and smoke, buy and smoke again. When I heard that, I couldn't help thinking what an odd business this was. You sold people something that they took home and burned, then immediately sold them more.

For a few days the media descended on Colorado, beaming back salacious stories of our new favorite vice. A lot of people who were buying were quarter-ounce tourists, some of whom had flown in specifically to participate in what many considered a historic event. At about $300 an ounce, some shops were raking in close to $100,000 a day. Demand was so high that many dispensaries were hanging OUT OF STOCK signs in their windows before the weekend was over.

At our dispensaries, we were seeing a similar influx of newcomers, but all of them were turned away empty-handed. That's because I had made the decision early on that we were not going to rush into the recreational market just yet. We had the proper licenses to grow and sell recreationally, but I didn't think it was prudent to do so until the market had worked out some of the kinks.

To run a business that sells consumable products to the public, you must be ready to meet or exceed expectations and be able to maintain what you start. You cannot showcase the best weed in the world one week and then abysmal product the next week—or, worse, be out of stock. I see entering the consumer market like running a marathon. Before you do it, you want to make sure you have trained well, that your mind and your body are both ready for the challenge that lies before you, that you've outfitted yourself with the correct equipment, and that you are set up to succeed.

When you sell to medical marijuana customers, you're selling to a deliberately small market and can easily field newbie questions. Once a medical user is up and running on a marijuana regimen that works for him or her, it's easy to tweak what the person buys over time.

When you're selling to newbies off the street, you have one chance to win them over. You need to make sure your packaging is correct and that your customer service is flawless.

Those who rushed into the adult-use market were destined to make mistakes—and many did. Dispensaries sold buds and edibles to newbie marijuana consumers who went home and proceeded to have alarmingly uncomfortable experiences. At the time of this writing, I know of one company that has been hit with a class action suit because of this very issue. Because the company lacks product liability insurance, it probably will go under—all because of an easily avoidable mistake.

Because of this and a host of other ramp-up issues, I didn't think it was worth being the first to sell to this new market. As a result, a lot of people who walked into our shops in 2014 left disappointed. But I know it was the right decision to make.

Before the night of the election, I had worked through different scenarios and variables with the Green Man team in an attempt to know a little more about the great unknown that was facing us. I predicted that in order to meet the adult-use market, we would need more than four times our current production levels.

On that New Year's Day in 2014, legal marijuana was a novelty. The market was so new that it was impossible to judge just how many people ultimately would become regular buyers. At this point, an accurate number was unknowable. To meet the expected demand, the state was allowing growers to make a one-time-only transfer of their medical inventory to recreational inventory. If you wanted to grow fresh plants for the recreational market, you needed to apply for a new set of licenses.

That was fine, but still: Four times the plants? That meant more lights. More facilities. More grows. More employees to service all those new customers.

We weren't there yet and wouldn't be for a while, but I didn't mind running in the pack early in the race. I had a game plan, a vision, for how to win the weed game in Colorado. I knew if I stuck to my plan, we would be in front when we came to the finish line. Now, finally, it was time to build the Cannabis Ranch.

13

LOOKING FOR
THE WIN-WIN

THE BUSINESS WAS THRIVING AND GROWING, AND WE
were looking forward to the 2014 Cannabis Cup in Denver. In the
office, we buckled down and clarified the details of our booth at
that year's event, which had moved to a larger location at the Denver
Mart. That was followed up with our usual strain-selection party at
my place. The next morning, Barb, Corey, and I made the final six
picks.

There isn't a company on the planet that doesn't think twice
about whether they should participate in their industry's next trade
show. That's because it's always so hard to determine the immediate
benefit to spending lavishly to attend a particular event. When times
are great, companies tend to be freer with the budgets. When times
are tough, they retrench. But if we didn't make an appearance at the
first Cannabis Cup in the year marijuana went legal in our state, it
would be as if we didn't exist. So we went all out, booking a 20-by-
20-foot booth and erecting a custom-made Green Man tent nearest
the entrance to the event's smoking area. I had twenty-two people
working two shifts a day, lighting the company bong, selling a ton

of T-shirts, and getting happily baked outdoors with a lot of friendly faces.

We thought it would be smart to hand out munchies in that crowd. So anyone who came by the booth got a paper cup with our logo on it, stuffed with a (marijuana-free) serving of green-and-white-colored popcorn. By the end of the weekend, we had distributed twenty thousand servings of popcorn. If you looked out at the crowd, it seemed as if every person on the floor was walking around with a Green Man cup. I like to think we made an impression.

The third day of the 37,000-person event happened to land on Easter Sunday, and the trade show weekend coincided with a 420 event, a massive outdoor rally celebrating marijuana legalization that took place in the city's Civic Center Park, not far from the state capitol. The park was packed with 80,000 people. The marijuana-leaf bandanas and hemp clothing and marijuana edible kiosks were doing a brisk business.

So were the cops.

Remember: It was still illegal in Colorado to smoke marijuana in public. But despite the fact that police had posted signs to this effect throughout the park, ecstatic event goers largely ignored the ban. The cloud of marijuana smoke that hovered in front of the state capital was a taunt. The cops reacted well, I thought. If they saw you breaking the law right in front of their faces, they issued you a $150 fine. But by the end of the day, only twenty-two people had been arrested.

Across town at the Denver Mart, I was not nearly as clueless about the award program as I had been the first year we attended. I was in the room, listening, when the judges called our name.

Our Ghost Train Haze strain took the U.S. Cannabis Cup for best sativa. To look at it, it's not a terribly distinctive bud, but it gives off a rich, sharp, almost metallic smell. When you smoke it, you can taste that same metallic flavor. Its high is not incapacitating. Instead, you're overcome with a gentle, light euphoria that makes it a fine choice for newcomers.

A bunch of us in the back erupted with cheers. We ran up and took the stage. The presenters handed me the small cup, which was the highest award of that year's event. I waved it over my head and screamed, "Oh my God! We did it! We did it *again!*"

Scott Reach, the founder of a seed company called Rare Dankness and the breeder of Ghost Train Haze, was in the audience when our win was announced. He joined us on stage and joined in our celebration. We had won by growing his creation. It was good to have him on stage with us. Kim Sidwell, the de facto official photographer of the cannabis movement, snapped a picture of the Green Man team on stage together, accepting the award. That picture would end up in *High Times* magazine and today graces our conference room. It was one of my proudest moments because we'd won as a team.

We hadn't won in 2013, but we were okay with that. For most growers, the Cannabis Cup is a once-in-a-lifetime achievement. Which is why the 2014 award meant so much. We had won two of these in five years. We were doing something right.

As we were stepping down from the stage, some reporters were waiting to pull us aside. Could we go somewhere to talk? Would we let them film us for a short interview?

Fine, I said, and followed them out to the hallway to set up the shot.

I figured that they were with a local news program. Or part of the growing marijuana media that covered these events internationally. But they weren't.

"We're with *CBS This Morning,*" the producer said, and then before I had a chance to regain my composure over being interviewed by one of the nation's oldest and most respected morning programs, the lights came on, and the cameras started rolling. The following morning, before I'd had my coffee, I watched veteran broadcaster Charlie Rose introduce me to the nation as the man who grew the best marijuana in the country. That was nice, if not strictly accurate.

But then, you can't expect the media to nail down the details every single time.

Monday I had every intention of going into the office, but I was too exhausted from the previous week, so I just slept in. I woke to a backload of messages on my cellphone. My voicemail had been deluged with well-wishers, mainstream news reporters, cannabis industry journalists, and more, all of whom wanted to talk or get a quote.

Our accountant Patrick gave me the final tally of our costs for the weekend: $72,000. We had gone over budget, which is never fun. But I consoled myself with two things: (1) We had walked away with the event's top prize, and (2) we had staked out our claim with thousands of marijuana enthusiasts who had flown to Denver to attend this event. I could not put a price on that type of brand recognition. We wanted to attract exactly this demographic with the Cannabis Ranch in a few years.

It wasn't until a day or so later, down at one of the grows, that I got a chance to catch up with the man who is actually responsible for producing the best marijuana in the country—our grower Corey.

"Can I talk to you a sec?" he said. "It's kind of important."

He then launched into what was on his mind. I don't remember precisely how he phrased it, but it was in reference to a recent deal we were trying to work out with a potential partner in Nevada. This partner had enough pull to get itself a medical marijuana license in that state, but the owners had no desire to be weed farmers or retailers. They wanted to contract their day-to-day management to a company with a proven record. I had a lot riding on this deal. If our application was accepted, we'd have a shot at setting up a fresh operation in a second state.

And now, here was Corey, telling me he wasn't going to be able to put his name on the Nevada application. You see . . . he, uh. . . . had been working with someone else.

My face was warm.

You're my friend, I thought. *You can't do this to me.*

"Where are you going?" I asked him.

He mentioned the name of a start-up medical marijuana company in Nevada. He'd been in negotiations with them—and other outfits back home in Georgia and Florida—for more than four months. Nevada wanted him. Badly. And the owners were willing to give him a piece of their company. Six months ago, we had granted him an equity share of our business without requiring a financial commitment from him. We wanted him to feel part of the team.

And he was walking away from all this?

"You don't do this this way," I snapped. "You don't just *leave*. You could have come talked to me."

"I tried to, a couple of times. But when I mentioned the possibility of doing something outside Green Man, you said no."

He reminded me of several conversations we'd had, and he was correct. I had shut him down. I had not been open to hearing about any deal outside of Green Man, and Corey was itching to do something that would allow him to get a larger ownership position. He knew his time was ripe to grab the golden ring.

"You know what?" I said, "Let's do this later. When can we sit and talk?"

I was pissed. Fucking pissed.

I'd gone to bat for him to get equity in our company because he'd done amazing things for us. We had hammered out what I'd thought was a generous package for him. But it hadn't been enough, not compared to the other offers a man of his abilities can get at this time in this industry. Yet he had yessed me six months ago, the last time we talked about his future, and now it looked like he'd gone out shopping for a better deal.

There's no other way to put it. I felt betrayed. But I was just wise enough to realize that I was probably also just feeling vulnerable. In the last year, my wife and I had split; I had been betrayed then, and now the divorce was final. I had the feeling that I was wrongfully projecting the feelings I had about my broken marriage onto Corey's choices.

For a couple days, I thought about the Corey situation and realized that I had a chance to make it right. If I was honest with myself, I had to admit that I probably would have done the same thing in his position. I talked it out with Barb and Mr. Pink, and I came to understand how Corey had reached this point. Well, I thought, Corey wants to own a piece of something that corresponds to his contribution. He wants more, and he deserves it. He had helped me achieve my goals, and I would help him achieve his.

Late one afternoon, Corey was waiting for me when I got to El Diablo. I sat at the bar and ordered the usual: a Dos Equis and a shot of chilled Patrón. No training wheels—no lime, no salt.

"I'm not through being pissed at you," I told him. "But I get it. I feel like you lied to me. You should have told me."

"I tried—" And he again recounted all the times he had brought it up.

"I know. But, fuck, dude, we just won the fucking U.S. Cannabis Cup together, *again*. Are you fucking kidding me?"

Yeah, there was a lot of swearing. I put together a string of expletives that I would proudly look back upon later.

"Look," Corey said, "I'm sorry you found out the way you did. But I can't go on your Nevada application. My name is already on one which has been submitted, and no one person can be on two applications."

This was correct. This was going to make a lot of work for Barb and the team that was submitting the Nevada application. They had already written Corey into all the documents; removing him would compromise the quality of our document. But we had no choice.

"Can we just come clean for a second?" I said. "What do you want? What's the end goal right now?"

He seemed relieved that I had asked and launched into a longer explanation. He wanted a better future for himself and his family. He didn't want to wake up one day to find out that he was in his sixties and still working for the same cannabis company for a basic salary and a few points. He wanted to make something for himself.

"It's different for you," he said. "You already have a big equity stake in a big company. I don't. I don't want to work my whole life *for* someone like you. I want to *be* you. I want to be where you are."

He was basically echoing something that Brandon, one of my earliest growers, had said. The world of cannabis was opening up. Guys like Brandon and Corey had expertise that they knew was valuable, but they weren't sure how to go about selling it to the world.

What I also heard in his words was poverty consciousness— believing that you will always be trapped in a rat race where the wealth goes to the very few, which never includes you. I recognized the signs.

Corey and I had similar upbringings. We grew up with hardworking parents. And we were hard workers, hungry and resilient. I'd been working since I was eight years old, first on a newspaper route, then cleaning a women's resource center in Boulder where my mom volunteered and got them to hire my brother and me.

But over the years I'd internalized a radical message: The world is filled with unlimited wealth and opportunities. Why worry how much money you are making at *this* job? If you are unhappy, find your bliss. If you find a job that pays you more, do that. Or start a business because you're passionate about creating a new product. Quit your accounting job and start baking the best muffins in the world and sell them to local coffee shops. Do what you must, but find your bliss. The world is abundant when you are doing what you are here to do. I could tell Corey wanted to believe in this philosophy but was having trouble seeing it come to fruition.

I lifted the tequila to my lips and tossed it back.

In my head, I had a couple of thoughts: I like this guy. I like his family. He's a good, solid person, and I need to help him.

I reached over the bar for a napkin.

"What do you want to make?" I said, digging in my pocket for a pen. "A million, two million?"

He started protesting, probably assuming that I was making a joke. He knew our company couldn't afford to pay him that kind of salary.

"No," I said. "It's all gonna come from *you*. You don't just have skill. You have intellectual property. You're the man who knows how to grow the best weed in the world. So you don't go to work *for* these guys. You get them to sign a contract with you and you *consult* with them."

My pen was cranking out some numbers. What was he worth? Hell, what was he worth to *me* on the open market? A few hundred bucks an hour? A few hundred hours a month of his time?

"You just told me you know guys who could use you down in Florida and Georgia, right? Well, fine. They sign a contract with you, too. And then of course *I* sign a contract with you, too—"

"You would, too?" he said.

"After I get finished being pissed, yeah. Because I know you're worth it. See, if you do it this way, a couple of jobs like you do for me and then get a few other clients, in a year you could end up making . . ."

I held up the napkin.

"Jesus!"

"It won't be easy, but it's doable. But this way, your family doesn't have to move to Nevada. They stay put right here in Denver. You fly to the clients to dial in their growing operations. It stresses you, not your family. And one day, when you get sick of flying around and the business is established, you could probably sell it for, oh, six to ten million bucks."

He was silent, peering at the numbers on my napkin like they were unobtainable gold.

"I can't . . . I can't do that. I'm already in with these guys in Nevada. They're offering me forty percent of the company."

I smiled. "Do both. Look, I don't want to tell you what to do. But if you go to Nevada, you're moving backward. In four years' time, you'll still be running their *one* grow servicing their *one* dispensary, and the whole time, you'll have to keep praying that they know how to run a business. We'll have twenty dispensaries in three years' time. Why go backward? Play the field. Get us all to sign consulting agreements. That way, you get a piece of *all* our companies."

You could see in his eyes he was thinking, "This could work."

I slid the numbers over to him.

"Take the napkin home. Think about it. Want another drink?"

THURSDAY NIGHT, it was my board's turn to be pissed.

Who the hell did Corey think he was? He had already put his name on another application? For some other company? The ranting went on for a little while. The directors were all pissed. Similarly, they all felt betrayed. They had every right to be angry. They also had every right to be happy. My job was to get them to accept happy over angry.

If there's one thing I've learned, it's that fighting in business rarely gets you anywhere. You have to look for the win-win solution. If you're selling something, you have to figure out what the other guy needs, not only because he'll help you close the deal but because you'll have his emotional buy-in as well. With employees, the paradigm is slightly different. They want a good salary and benefits, but they also want to feel appreciated. They want to feel like part of a team, part of something bigger. That's where I'd screwed up with Corey. I'd ignored his requests to talk about his future, and I'd made him feel like he was outside the fold.

"No," I told the board, "you're not seeing the whole picture. Corey is part of our success. He's part of the Green Man story. We either choose to be angry, or we can choose to have a meaningful business partnership."

They came around slowly, but they came around. When we adjourned the meeting, the board was on board. I just needed to wait for Corey's response to my proposal.

People often need to be reminded what side their bread is buttered on. I was pretty sure we were going to work something out with Corey. He knew my offer was sincere and heartfelt, and he would consider it carefully. But I also felt good for myself. I had managed to sever my feelings of work betrayal from the bullshit of my personal life. And I had taken a positive step forward to appreciate a colleague I loved like a brother, and who had helped make my business what it was.

Later that week, we threw a party at the Cap City Tavern to congratulate ourselves on the Cannabis Cup win. We invited everyone we could think of—employees, board members, vendors, colleagues, patients, and clients. In the back of the bar, we set up a bar of our own. Instead of serving drinks, we were offering samples of our winning Ghost Train Haze and all of the other strains we had showcased at the Cannabis Cup. Our guests helped themselves to our bud bar.

We all marveled at our new world as we smoked away.

I got roped into a conversation with a marijuana hater.

"I still think it's wrong," she told me bluntly. She had hated seeing the national media cover the 420 event in front of the capitol. Hated seeing her city broadcast nationally as the marijuana mecca of the United States. "I just think it's bad publicity and it's bad for the state."

Hey, I wanted to say, your husband has been working with our company for five years. You're directly benefiting from our success.

And thank you for your concern, I could have gone on, but I think the great state of Colorado is making out all right in the bargain. Last I checked, it was projecting a $30 million windfall this year on marijuana tax revenue.

But hey—she is entitled to her point of view. If she says she doesn't like seeing Denver portrayed this way, who can argue?

It's not my place to judge what other people think or feel. As I'd just recently learned for the umpteenth time, even when I think I am in a fully committed relationship, my partners may change their minds. It reminded me to choose my partners carefully and remain flexible. With all our success, there remained many hurdles, both expected and unexpected, to be overcome.

I nodded until she wandered off to procure more of her drug of choice—booze.

14

INVESTORS

SOMETIME IN 2013, I BEGAN PUTTING TOGETHER BUSIness plans to present to the qualified investors I was courting. Every business plan has a section where the prospective borrower states the risks of investing in their company. Typically, the biggest risk is that investors might well lose their shirts. Ours was probably the only business plan ever written that carried this strange disclaimer:

> *Currently, there are many drug dealers and cartels that cultivate, buy, sell and trade marijuana in Colorado and worldwide. Many of these dealers and cartels are violent and dangerous as well as well-financed and well-organized. It is possible that these dealers and cartels could feel threatened by legalized marijuana businesses such as the Company's and could take action against or threaten the Company, its principals, employees and/or agents, and this could negatively impact the Company and its business.*

The language is pure Wall Street: measured, careful, perhaps even a little stilted, but I'm guessing you get the gist. Now, did I really believe that there was a slight chance that drug lords were going to come kill us? No. According to the last report I'd read, the United States' illegal drug habit—for all major drugs—generated about $100 billion for the drug cartels every year. The entire *legal* marijuana business in the United States took in only $1.53 billion in revenue in 2013. By that measure, I thought the drug lords were still doing pretty well, but there was still a risk, and every risk needs to be in a business plan.

When I was fresh out of college and starting my first ice cream shop, a young friend of mine had a sizable fortune and wanted to invest in my business. I was into it. She was gung-ho. There was just one hurdle. Her accountant wanted to see my business plan.

I was like, *Huh?*

I had graduated college with a BA in political science. I had studied Russian and traveled to Russia as part of my education. My first trip was part of a language and cultural exchange to Leningrad in the summer of 1990. My second trip was to Moscow in the summer of 1992. I arrived in a very different place than I had been two years before. The Russian people had revolted against the communists who controlled the Soviet Union. Once their revolt turned to revolution, they installed a democratically elected senate and president. It was a fascinating moment in history for a young man to observe.

While in college, I was president of my fraternity, SAE, vice president of the student body government, president of the student senate, vice president of College Republicans, and sat on a Greek disciplinary board. I was one of those serious young people who got quoted a lot in the campus newspaper. I was a big man on campus, maybe too big. I was a straight-C student. The whole time I was in college, I was learning a lot about how the world worked. In addition to the activities I just mentioned, I always held down another job to pay the bills. I worked as a bartender, a caddy, and a bouncer at a topless bar.

But I'd never written a business plan.

I wouldn't get my friend's money unless I did. So I went to the library, read up on some models of what these plans looked like, went back to my apartment in Seattle, and cranked one out in a weekend.

I got the money and ran that ice cream business for five years before selling what I had grown into a three-store local chain.

It wasn't until later, when I was working for a start-up mortgage bank, that I finally grasped what kind of information investors needed to hear in order to close the deal. The institutional investors I was dealing with were serious. There was little room in their cosmology for passion. These guys weren't investing because they loved real estate. Their jobs were to deploy this capital and get the anticipated return, and if I wanted them to take me seriously, I had to speak their language.

Following a brief introduction to the concept of the investment, we would provide them with an information memorandum (IM) that explained the proposed investment in great detail. IMs are the cheat sheets of the business world. They give a detailed description of the nature of the investment, the management team, financial projections (historical as well as forward-looking pro forma financials), risk factors (like the drug cartels mentioned earlier) as well as a host of supporting exhibits—the operating agreement, subscription agreement, investor questionnaire, and so on. The intention is to provide investors with all the information they need to make an investment decision in as few pages as possible.

In my new life as a ganjapreneur, I was beginning to see that I had a leg up on so many of my competitors. They were growing weed because they had been in the business before it went legit, or they had gotten hit by the recession and were looking to do something else. But they didn't have business backgrounds. All they knew was that cannabis was fun and looked to be a hell of a lot less stressful than the rat race they'd just fled. Some of the owners of these dispensaries thought it distasteful to hustle and grow their business. They wanted to take it easy. Perhaps they even regarded cannabis as the slow path to a comfortable retirement. Many had gotten in early with dollar signs in their eyes. They imagined arising each morning to a new sack of cash being delivered to them by magical fairies, only to wake from their dream state to realize that the marijuana business was as complicated and competitive as any business out there.

The trouble was, the industry was constantly changing.

At this time, everywhere I turned, people wanted to take a meeting to talk investment opportunities. I was doing meetings with long-time Colorado residents, meetings with out-of-towners, meetings with rich guys who were looking to set up their sons or daughters in a business that they wouldn't screw up, meetings with semiretired country clubbers who wanted to brag to their friends that they still had skin in the game and were shifting their portfolio beyond boring blue-chip stocks.

In some of those meetings were polished individuals who worked for the Big Tobacco companies. They were watching the cannabis industry very closely. For now, they were prevented by law from investing in the marijuana business in states like Colorado, but those restrictions would lapse soon enough, and these companies would descend upon our market with their entire arsenal. They had everything they needed to succeed: lobbyists, politicians amenable to their cause, farmers willing to grow the next big crop at a moment's notice, and a shitload of money. One guy I talked to let slip that his tobacco company already had an outdoor grow facility in the Southeast, just waiting for marijuana to become legal there.

It did not shake me up at all to think that someday you'd walk into a 7-Eleven and be able to buy a pack of joints as easily as cigarettes. That was inevitable. It troubled me more that these guys might possibly take an industry that prided itself on growing with integrity—cleanly, naturally, organically wherever possible—and turn marijuana into a pesticide-heavy crop. Most of the growers I knew denied that such a thing would ever happen, but I could feel it in my bones. Like it or not, brutally efficient capitalism will eventually transform what has been until now a very mom-and-pop, feel-good industry.

The numbers also suggested that the cannabis industry was already constricting. In our state, the number of licensed retailers had declined by 40 percent in the first few years. That suggested that people were rushing into the business, losing their shirts, and not being replaced. If your cannabis company was not growing, you already needed to start thinking about who you might sell to as an escape strategy.

Many of the dispensary and grow owners I've met have been lucky to attract money from outside investors, but they are ill-equipped to deal with the ramifications of that new obligation. I am still surprised when I meet people who are running successful cannabis companies who don't understand the difference between getting a loan and selling equity in their business. I'm not being facetious. They don't understand that they are selling a portion of their company, and maybe even control of the company, in exchange for a much-needed infusion of capital. I finally had to take one friend aside after he shared an agreement he had signed with a "lender" and say, "Dude, you understand that they own a piece of your company?"

"No, I'm just going to pay him back and then give him like twenty grand or something for his help."

"No, this agreement gives him equity ownership in your company, and if you fail to make a payment to him, he can take control of the business."

I didn't know what to tell him. Welcome to Business 101, maybe?

Still, I looked forward to describing our opportunity to more sophisticated investors. I had internalized the examples of a couple of good role models.

I admired Ben & Jerry's greatly. Have you ever noticed that customers aren't just loyal to the Ben & Jerry's brand? They're loyal to the *flavor*. I've overheard arguments between people over what flavor they should get at the supermarket to take home tonight. Chunky Monkey? Cherry Garcia? Hazed & Confused? New York Super Fudge Chunk? Phish Food? People swear by those flavors, and they know they can't get them from any other brand. Think about how unusual that is. You might well love coffee, but are you loyal to French roast? I believed we could get people loyal to SkunkBerry, Ghost Train Haze, and Hells OG Kush.

The other thing I admired about Ben & Jerry's is that it transcended what the average corporation was supposed to be about. Companies aren't supposed to have souls or personalities, but Ben & Jerry's always did, even before it was fashionable.

Starbucks is another company that inspires intense brand loyalty. Yeah, I know—not everyone loves its coffee; not everyone loves that the shops are on every street corner in America. But you cannot deny that, for many people, that first sip of Starbucks was their first inkling that coffee could be a luxury product, a cut above the swill served in most fast-food locations in America until that time. Howard Schultz, the CEO who took Starbucks to the next level, is one of my role models in this regard, a classic Wall Street capitalist who managed to excite enough investors to raise the billions he needed to literally grow a store a day.

I wanted to create the same public passion for marijuana.

I wanted to grow the company in an honorable way.

I wanted Green Man Cannabis to be different from other marijuana out there. I wanted to win the minds, then the hearts, and finally the wallets of marijuana product and lifestyle consumers and become the most recognized brand of legal marijuana in the world.

Bold? Yes. In front of me was a great opportunity to achieve everything I had ever wanted. This was Green Man's moment, and I was completely committed to capturing it. And I was going to do it in a way that was meaningful.

As soon as the recreational-use referendum passed, I started getting calls out of the blue from potential investors who were eager to get in on the ground floor of the marijuana industry.

I was grateful. The first phase of our Cannabis Ranch construction required about $25 million in capital. A guy who needs money for his business can't afford to pass up any opportunity to get someone to write him a check.

But this newfound attention quickly became a double-edged sword. I had underestimated how much education would be involved in wooing investors. When I was in real estate, I didn't have to teach people what real estate was, or how it was "made," or what we did with it. Everyone knew the score. God made land, and he wasn't making more of it.

Legal cannabis was different. My typical song and dance with a potential investor started with my monologue about the industry. They had tons of questions: How profitable is it? Can I get in? What are the pluses? What are the downsides? And finally: What's an opportunity with you look like?

Individual investors came to us with a lot of curiosity and passion. They wanted to make money *and* look cool in front of their friends. Institutional investors were curious, too, but they checked their passion at the door. They were all about the dollars. Would the cannabis industry lead to profits—or was it a waste of time?

Both types of investors had to jump through our state's legal loops. Direct investors had to be permanent residents of Colorado. That eliminated most of the people I talked to, but there were always some surprises.

An attorney friend of Mr. Pink's called me once, asking if I wouldn't mind spending some time talking to her about the Colorado cannabis industry in general. She had clients who were thinking of investing, but she knew nothing about the industry at all. Her approach was guarded, but she was willing to learn in order to be better able to advise her clients. Would I be willing to talk?

We had a single, hour-long call in which I gave her the lay of the land. I described where I thought the industry could be in five or ten years, purposely keeping my own fund-raising need out of the conversation. I was doing Mr. Pink a favor; calls like this were about educating a serious party, not making a pitch.

In the end, though, she didn't think the risks of the marijuana business were suited to the client she had in mind. She then asked if I knew of any other deals in the marijuana industry. I told her about ours, but she didn't think ours was right for her client, either. But there was *another* client of hers, a basketball player, who she thought might be a potential investor.

"He loves the idea of the marijuana business," she said. "He just can't get into it right now. He's still playing."

I knew what she was talking about. I had already met with a number of athletes who were in the same situation. Most of their contracts and sponsorship deals carried serious morality clauses. This was intended to make sure that these athletes projected a squeaky-clean image before the public. They couldn't be caught doing anything illegal. They had to stay clear of marijuana.

Here's where the hypocrisy of this stuff comes in. An actor, athlete, or other celebrity can be more easily forgiven by the media and public if he is TMZed dancing drunk and naked on a friend's roof than if he is busted with an ounce of marijuana intended for personal consumption. Our current political and cultural landscape is out of sync with reality and in need of reform. Which sometimes puts me in the ridiculous position of marijuana investment career counselor to the stars.

"You probably want to wait until you retire from the NBA," I told one athlete. "Whatever you could make from investing in our company is not worth losing your shoe deal over, not to mention your career." He reluctantly agreed.

Well, I finally met the ball player whom I'll simply describe as Mr. Tall. He didn't waste any time telling me how much he loved marijuana but never touched the stuff during the season. There was actually only a three-month window every summer when he could happily smoke weed without having to worry about a drug test from the NBA. Like a lot of athletes, he used weed for a variety of reasons.

It didn't cloud his head the way alcohol did. If he was hurting from an injury or just looking to comfort some aches, the drug's analgesic properties worked wonders. Above all, it helped him relax and sleep in a way that alcohol never would.

Mr. Tall was a state resident. And I liked him, so much so that we ended up working out a deal that will get him involved when he retires. But he's itching to do so now. In fact, every time he hears we are having some kind of event, he tells me how much he wishes he could be a part of it.

It was just his pain-in-the-ass multimillion-dollar basketball contract that was keeping him from being a part of our day to day. "Chris, man," he likes to say. "I tell you, as soon as I retire, I'm going to be there for you and Green Man. Anything you want. The Cannabis Cup, any event you're at, I'm there. I'm going to be lighting bongs for people at the booth."

THE MUSICIAN KNOWN AS REDMAN gave me a big hug when he entered the room and settled into a couch to start our meeting. I knew him only by reputation. He is a legendary figure in hip-hop, a Jersey-born rapper who has cut numerous records with his partner in rhyme, Method Man.

We met in Denver at the office of a mutual friend. Redman wasn't a Colorado resident, but he was passionate as hell. He and Method Man were often photographed smoking fat joints or displaying Ziploc bags filled with monster buds.

We got down to business. The conversation took its twists and turns but finally got around to the real reason we were meeting. Redman was looking to capitalize on the cannabis business. He'd liked what he'd seen of our operation, and he wanted in. There was just one thing that would clinch the deal for him.

He wanted us to name a strain after him. And he wanted it available for his fans to buy by the time his next album came out. That would be tricky.

"I don't have a problem naming something after you," I told him. "We could rename something that you yourself love. The bigger problem is, the only fans that would be able to buy it are those who live in or visit Colorado. That's probably not worth it for you. You're looking for a national platform. Plus you can't make money from it. That would qualify you as an owner, and you don't qualify for that because of your residency status."

"How do we get it outside Colorado?"

I shook my head. "We don't."

"You can't mail it?"

"Not without breaking a dozen different federal laws, no."

"Oh."

THE GUY I'LL CALLED SEÑOR DUFFEL was also excited about the cannabis industry. He'd seen our name around town, and he was ready to jump in feet first.

"I could probably invest a million to start."

"A million dollars?" I was impressed by how casually and assuredly he said it. A million dollars was always welcome. It would speed up my capital campaign enormously.

"One catch," he said. "It's a million cash. We'll deliver it to you in a duffel bag. But you'll have to be responsible for laundering it."

Oh shit.

"Laundering? Uh, no," I said. "It doesn't work like that. It has to be completely legal. We have to file an affidavit for every single dime we take in. We must be able to trace this back to a legitimate source."

"You mean to say, you're, like, completely legit?"

"That's right."

"Oh."

THE GUY I'LL CALL BORIS was a millionaire many times over who owned and operated mines in various locations in Eastern Europe.

He wanted to invest. But he also wasn't a resident of Colorado. In fact, you could say he wasn't a resident of anywhere. This oligarch traveled by private jet to reach his various mining enterprises and the meetings he took all over the world.

He spent a lot of his life on that plane, smoking his way through copious quantities of marijuana at 33,000 feet.

"WHAT DOES THE BIBLE say about this?"

I was sitting with a group of investors, all of whom were devout Christians. They were open to these new opportunities, but they weren't sure the Bible condoned marijuana.

Some activists have argued that marijuana actually appears in the Bible as the "aromatic" or "sweet cane" mentioned in the Old Testament. Some say that cannabis is one of the ingredients in the holy anointing oil used by ancient Hebrews and early Christians. Naturally, traditional biblical scholars dispute these assertions.

I always try to be respectful about this topic. I'm not devout in the traditional sense, but many people in my extended family are. My aunt is a fundamentalist Christian, and my study of this topic grew largely out of my desire to explain my business motives to people like her.

"Have you read the Bible or the Torah? Do you believe in its guidance?" I usually ask. Nearly always, religious folks say that they have read one of these books and that they find its guidance meaningful.

"Yes, of course," they might say.

That's when I refer them to the words the Lord spoke on the Sixth Day, quoting Genesis 1:29:

Then God said, "Behold, I have given you every plant yielding seed that is on the surface of all the earth, and every tree which has fruit yielding seed; it shall be food for you . . ."

I HAD TWO LARGE INVESTORS interested in helping us build the Cannabis Ranch. One was William, the Wichita investor I mentioned earlier. Another was a private equity firm based in New York City. Their firm had about $4 billion under management. If we were going to get the Cannabis Ranch built, I needed these two investors to come in as partners in the larger real estate deal. They would buy the land, build the facility, and lease it to us. By acting as our landlords, they would neatly sidestep the state law preventing non-residents from investing in marijuana businesses. They would never own a share of the company, but they would share in our success by renting to us.

For much of 2014, I was immersed in visits and conference calls with my attorney and accountant and theirs. One of those parties still had issues with the numbers.

At the time we were talking, twenty-two states had legalized some form of medical marijuana. Two—Colorado and Washington—were rolling out recreational use. It was just a matter of time, I told them, before other states moved forward with recreational use. When that happened, I envisioned building a Cannabis Ranch in those states as well.

Wait, someone from the New York team said: You don't mean to apply for a license to grow in those states?

No, I said. I don't have to. We'll build the Cannabis Ranch and then we'll go to the top ten license holders in the state and ask one to partner with us. They'll sign a lease with us, but to do it, they must agree to grow to Green Man's specifications and use the Green Man logo on all their products.

Entering other states as a license holder was already becoming tricky. I knew because we had tried. But it occurred to me that we didn't need to play in that sandbox if all I was doing was buying, developing, and renting a state-of-the-art marijuana facility. The first license holder who was smart enough to sign with us would be ahead of the curve. He or she would have access to the first marijuana agritourism facility in the state that was linked to a nationwide chain of promotion.

Oh, the New York investors said, nodding. Then *you* become the brand.

Exactly.

Those deals took months to put together and taught me much about the benefits of cultivating patience. Staying present in each moment, with each breath. Breathe in, breathe out.

That summer I decided to take a few days off and fly to Cabo San Lucas, at the tip of the Baja peninsula, for a short vacation. I never seemed to get enough quiet time at the office those days. I'd discovered that I got more done with a laptop and a cell phone in Mexico than I did in Colorado.

My personal life had changed dramatically. Following my recent divorce, I was in a new relationship with a woman, Rebecca, who had two children of her own. We'd taken a trip that weekend for some quiet time alone.

I was sitting by the pool one morning when William and his team called. We went through some chitchat, and then I heard his advisor, Justin, pause for breath. The pause I was waiting for. The pause that said "You've answered all our questions and we need to share some news with you."

"We're ready to commit," Justin said. "We're ready to come in at $5 million. We believe you have a solid business and a great plan; we are excited to be part of it. How soon can we close?"

Yessssss!

We talked for a little while longer, discussing the steps necessary to close and the timelines.

The next morning, I was on the phone with the private equity firm in New York. The last time I'd seen its offices, I was standing in a temple of glass and steel high above Madison Avenue. The glossy prospectus on the coffee table in front of me said that one of the prominent members of their board of directors was a former state governor; another was a legendary athlete. The rap on companies like this was that it was sometimes easier to get $100 million out of them than what I needed: $4 million.

It took them a while to get my contact on the phone.

"Hey, how are you?"

"Fine. I don't want to keep you," I said. "I just wanted to let you know I got a commitment of $5 million from William yesterday."

"We heard."

Of course they had.

"Tell you what," my contact said. "We're ready to do business. We're ready to come in at $4 million."

Yessssss!

There was the usual promise of paperwork, the inspection of our documentation, the due diligence period. There were the obvious concerns about our current, all-cash position. The firm was prepared to hire an auditor on a regular basis to make sure the cash didn't get out of control. If all went well, my contact said the firm could see helping us take the business public someday. And my contact thought the firm could manage an additional $1 million, earmarked for dispensaries I might want to buy along the way.

It was all good.

I hung up the phone and pounded the air with my fist.

"Did they say yes, too?" Rebecca said with a smile.

"Yes," I said.

I had commitments for $9 million from two institutional investors.

Two commitments in twenty-four hours.

For a marijuana business.

All while sitting by a pool in Mexico.

It was a good day. A very, very good day.

15

THE NEW MARIJUANA ECONOMY

ONE NIGHT NOT LONG AGO, I ATTENDED A POLITICAL fund-raiser for the governor of Colorado hosted by a handful of ganjapreneurs, myself included, in downtown Denver. Those evenings are always glittering events. People dressed to the nines. Lots of handshakes, hugs, and photographs. Endless rounds of cocktails and equally endless rounds of speeches. But I have to admit that for part of the time, my mind was elsewhere. I was busy looking around the room, counting up how many of those people were cannabis entrepreneurs like me. These were people I'd done business with. People who ran major grows or dispensaries. People who had entered the field when it was still in its clumsy infancy, who had ridden the ups and downs and had emerged unscathed on the other side.

I had to marvel that our state's top politicians would even want us there. Once, having known drug dealers show up at such an event would have been an anathema. A scourge. Something worthy of scandal. Such a person would have been shown the door, escorted out, or quietly arrested outside. And now our presence was welcome. We were, in fact, the hosts and had invited all the guests. Politicians wanted our votes, our support, and our donations.

I had another thought as well. I found myself thinking: The Steve Jobs of marijuana is *here*. I don't know who he or she is, but they're in this room right now. And, no doubt, somewhere in Washington state, at a similar party in the future, the Jeff Bezos or Howard Schultz of marijuana will be in attendance. In the coming years, the major players of this new industry are going to emerge, and they will surprise the larger world of business with their achievements.

Now, you might well mock such a gathering as an assemblage of highly privileged people. *Of course* the big shots are going to welcome major marijuana businesspeople to the fold. They're eager to get a hold of your tax dollars! They want your money, dude!

Yeah, I get it.

But I also think that you don't have to look far to find evidence that Colorado's stance on marijuana has mellowed, not just for us entrepreneurs but for *everyone*.

In fact, the night of this party, my head was still coming to terms with a story a friend had told me at lunch. A neighbor had called the cops to complain about a strange smell emanating from a home in my friend's neighborhood. When the cops arrived, they found two young men who were growing more than 170 plants on the premises. Each had a red card showing that his physician had approved them for a higher plant count, should he choose to grow his own. However, under the new recreational marijuana laws, they were only permitted to grow six plants each for personal consumption, and the city of Denver does not allow more than a total of twelve plants in any one home. You might say that three separate authorities—the physician, the state, and the city—all conflicted with each other.

In the past, the discovery of such a home grow would have brought out the feds in riot gear. The young men would have been arrested, indicted, found guilty, and done hard time. You will recall that when I was first interviewing growers in 2009, I met a young man who had just been released from prison after eight years. That young fellow's life was ruined because he had dared to grow this plant.

What was the result of the bust my friend told me about? The cops confiscated (and destroyed) all but twelve plants, issued the men a ticket for a smell violation—yes, there is such a thing—amounting to a few hundred dollars, and bade them a fine day.

Another person I know had a fascinating experience. He was going through security at the Denver airport. After his carry-on had gone through the X-ray screener, the security officer asked to open his Dopp kit, in which he kept all his toiletries.

"What do you have in here?" the airport screener asked.

My friend froze. Before he'd left home, he'd forgotten to remove certain items that he knew he was not allowed to travel with.

"I'm sorry," he told the officer. "I have some marijuana and a big tube of toothpaste in there."

What was the response? The security officer confiscated the toothpaste—it was over the TSA's three-ounce size limit—and sent him on his way.

I am not kidding.

What a difference a decade makes. What a more reasonable, humane response.

If you're a hard-ass, you might well say that the people in both these stories got off easy. They *should* have been arrested and thrown in jail. To which I respond: Really? In a world that's mired with war, famine, poverty, disease—problems that are taxing the resources and intelligence of all nations—don't we have more important things to do than busting people who want to get high?

I think it's safe to say that the next decade will be filled with more surprises as we witness the rise of our new marijuana economy. None of us has a crystal ball, but here are some predictions going forward that I feel comfortable making.

CONSOLIDATION IS INEVITABLE

As I write this, it's estimated that there are about five hundred dispensaries in the state of Colorado. In five years' time, there will be fewer than three hundred dispensaries, operated by fewer, larger, and more capable marijuana companies. It's only logical that stronger firms will buy out the locations of smaller firms, assume their licenses, and rebrand those locations. This pattern will occur throughout the United States wherever marijuana becomes medically and/or recreationally legal.

Starting new retail locations from the ground up is time-consuming, and smart entrepreneurs will want to cut to the chase. Why go through the laborious process of applying for a license from the state, searching for retail space, building out that location, hiring new employees when you can simply buy out your smaller competitors?

The great investor Warren Buffett defines capitalism as "the ability to deploy capital." To my mind, this means acting in the most efficient manner possible to get a good return. Buying out the competition looks like an expensive way to go, but if you spend $100 million on a few dozen dispensaries, rebrand them, resulting in a more visible chain now worth more than $300 million, you have gained more by taking the more expensive route.

You'll also sidestep the headaches that come from starting a new location from scratch. In one case, while trying to enter the market in the ski town of Frisco, Colorado, I lost precious months trying to establish a new retail location, only to have the city council call a meeting specifically to rezone in order to eliminate marijuana dispensaries. We spent months and lots of money on that deal before the city council changed the ordinance. If you buy an existing operation, precedent is on your side.

LICENSING WILL BECOME TOUGHER AND MORE EXPENSIVE, FAVORING EARLY PLAYERS

The current cannabis industry is like *Little House on the Prairie*— small log homes and farms with a dusty Main Street dotted with shops and churches. The future of cannabis will ultimately look like a massive twenty-first-century megalopolis.

Corporatization of the marijuana industry has already begun.

When I got into the business in 2009, I was just coming off a financially devastating corporate bankruptcy and had little capital to invest. Luckily, all I had to do was send in my paperwork to the state, declaring that I was a caregiver, and then start shopping around for warehouse space with a friendly landlord. Back then the cost of starting a new grow or dispensary was in the neighborhood of $10,000 to $1 million, depending on what you were willing to risk. Today, if you want to start a dispensary in Aurora, a pleasant suburb of Denver, you must demonstrate access to more than $400,000 in liquid assets just to apply for a license to sell or grow.

Expect a similar pattern to occur throughout the United States. Cities and states will welcome marijuana companies, but they'll do it on their terms. They'll want the revenue, but they'll have little patience for small-time operators. Their preference will be for firms that are well heeled, organized, responsible—firms that will be able to start earning and remitting taxes as quickly as possible.

I'm dismayed to say that many states are currently awarding medical marijuana licenses only to associates of those in power. If these entrepreneurs aren't smart about their hiring and cultivation practices, they stand to lose big when their states move to recreational use and national brands become dominant. Serious marijuana connoisseurs will always gravitate to quality. Those who rush into the business thinking it's a guarantee for a quick buck will lose their shirts.

BRAND EXTENSION THROUGH THE STATES
WILL FOLLOW CONSOLIDATION

Why is it that you can walk into a liquor store and buy one bottle of fermented grape juice for $15 and another bottle for $200? Both of those bottles contain the same intrinsic product, don't they? Well, they do and they don't. Understanding the difference is the key to understanding how the marijuana industry will evolve.

When our grow facility was robbed and we lost some of our product, I was forced to buy some buds wholesale from other growers in order to meet my dispensary demands. Guess what? Our customers not only knew that something had changed about our product—they complained about it! We had been in business only a few years at the time, but our customers had already become loyal to the taste and quality of our product.

Right now marijuana is a commodity, like cotton, pork bellies, and oil. In general, most buyers don't really know or care who's growing, packaging, or selling the buds on the market. But that will inevitably change—and quickly.

All this consolidation has an end goal: establishing brand recognition. The firms that establish a consumer affinity—the magic combination of quality product, locations, packaging, pricing, and service—will own the largest slice of the pie.

Some of these brands will extend across state lines. Imagine you are flying from Pennsylvania to Las Vegas. You spot a package of Green Man SkunkBerry for sale in a Vegas dispensary. You remember enjoying the quality of that product and strain during a ski trip you took to Colorado last winter. Because of brand loyalty, you spring for that package over all other strains available. Nearly everything we buy in our lives is brand centered. Marijuana will follow. The brands that come out on top will reach the largest audience.

How that will happen is still up in the air. Currently legal marijuana cannot leave the state in which it is grown. But there are lots of different ways to grow a business. Starbucks is vertically integrated; the parent company roasts the beans and sells them out of stores that it owns and operates. McDonald's franchises. Budweiser sells its product to distributors who sell to stores. Ultimately, the market will decide which model makes the most sense.

RECREATIONAL MARIJUANA WILL
EXPAND DRAMATICALLY BY 2020

As I write this, medical marijuana is legal in twenty-five states and the District of Columbia. But not all bureaucracies governing those medical systems are created equal. Some work well, others don't. Moving to recreational would simplify matters enormously. By 2020, we could see ten to fifteen states making the leap to recreational marijuana. There will always be opposition, but reasonable voters and legislators only need to see evidence that it can be done prudently. States like Colorado and Washington are amassing convincing data every day on the positive impact of legalization on a state's economy and welfare. This data will persuade other states to legalize recreational marijuana.

MARIJUANA DOSING WILL BECOME STANDARDIZED

The marijuana we grow today is nearly eight times more potent than what was smoked at Woodstock. When most people first smoke our marijuana, they take one to two hits, tops. Smoking an entire joint would be like drinking a half case of beer. The evolution of marijuana sales will not be toward stronger marijuana but to *consistently dosed servings*. Consumers will want to know that they can smoke one joint and not be a complete wreck, just as consumers know that 1 ounce of spirits, 5 ounces of wine, and 12 ounces of beer all have approximately the same intoxicating effect. Similar standards will be created for marijuana dosing. Those guidelines should be created and adhered to by the industry. We should not wait to be forced to do this by a government agency. We know we need this and should proactively make it happen.

MARIJUANA MUST BECOME LEGAL ON
THE FEDERAL LEVEL—AND WILL

The *New York Times* and other major newspapers have already called for legalization of marijuana, citing scientific evidence that the risks are negligible when compared to tobacco and alcohol. At the moment, marijuana legalization isn't a priority for federal lawmakers. Both Congress and the White House appear to be quietly watching which way voters swing on the issue and how state legalization efforts impact voter resistance. Everyone's against it, until they're not. We just need to wait for the tipping point. Ultimately, the lure of tax money, the demands of sick patients, and the evidence that recreational rollouts have gone all too well will prove too overwhelming to ignore. That's when DC will take comprehensive action to address federal marijuana laws. That's when lawmakers will change regulations at the numerous federal agencies that have written the failed drug war rhetoric into their charters.

BANKING AND TAX LAWS MUST CHANGE—AND WILL

The banking and tax issues need to be resolved immediately. But sadly, as long as the cannabis industry consists primarily of small firms, we can expect to be ignored by Congress. When enough billion-dollar, private equity firms or large corporations are investing in marijuana, Congress will be unable to ignore the industry any longer. But we can't wait for that time.

Like it or not, Congress must act soon on banking. It should allow banks to offer account services to qualified firms, provided the banks vet those cannabis companies on a case-by-case basis and insist upon transparency in all their business dealings. And Congress should clarify the tax relationship of these corporations with the federal government. Being able to remit our taxes electronically to the federal government is fine; being *required* to remit our taxes electronically and not having access to the bank account needed to do so is not.

FOR BETTER OR WORSE, CORPORATE PENETRATION INTO THE MARIJUANA MARKET IS INEVITABLE

We already know Big Tobacco, Big Agra, and Big Pharma are watching the cannabis industry closely. They know it's going to be profitable, and they want in. Each has its own agenda—and corporate exploitation of the plant will not always be pretty.

The charm of the industry as it currently exists is that a customer can walk into a dispensary, buy something to smoke, and know the provenance of that product. Chances are, that product will have been locally produced and nurtured in the most natural way possible, with minimal pesticide use. That is likely to change if large tobacco companies start producing marijuana.

Big Agra will want to enter this field in much the same way that it has infiltrated key crops—corn, soy, potatoes, and the like—in the United States. Expect to see a Big Ag corporation patent the genetic sequence of several marijuana strains. If legal marijuana in the United States ever makes the leap to being grown outdoors on a large scale, which is conceivable, we can expect agriculture technology firms to develop bacteria- and pest-resistant strains. The thought of genetically modified marijuana may seem laughable to longtime marijuana users, but that day is probably coming.

Big Pharma firms are already arguing that the plant is too powerful to be left in the hands of civilians at medical marijuana dispensaries. They want to be able to lock down marijuana so they can generate lab-grown substitutes. Sadly, they may win over a new generation of physicians with expensive new medications, by promising better control over dosing and titration.

Yet part of marijuana's simple beautiful dance with humankind is that nothing more is required. The plant, humans, and fire—that is all. Just because we can control some aspect of the plant better doesn't mean we should. Big Pharma makes drugs; God created marijuana. Whom do you trust?

DRUG LORDS WILL MOVE ON

This is a huge guess on my part. It's hard to imagine a world where marijuana is no longer demonized and no longer the best-selling street drug. But it's coming. We just don't know what form it will take. Most people assume that drug lords won't bother smuggling marijuana into the United States because the current street market as we know it will evaporate. Consumers will chase the quality, convenience, and safety of brand strains. The theory is that drug dealers and cartels will move aggressively into harder drugs, such as cocaine, heroin, and meth. But what if they try to get creative by going legit? We have already seen cases, in medical marijuana states, where drug lords have funneled money to legal marijuana operations for warehouse grow construction. In the case I'm thinking of, law enforcement uncovered the scheme, and the attorney and entrepreneurs who accepted the tainted money faced criminal charges.

MARIJUANA WILL BE A GROWTH INDUSTRY

I'm constantly amazed by the number of people who ask me how their profession can help us grow our business. A man whose company manufactures cardboard boxes recently approached me, asking what kind of paperboard packaging we use on our materials. "None," I told him. "We're still using plastic bags." An executive of a large commercial bakery scheduled a meeting to talk about how their firm should plan for the future of marijuana-laced baked goods. Both of these calls led to productive conversations.

These entrepreneurs are not alone. I meet yoga instructors, physical therapists, and home care nurses who want to talk about how marijuana can be incorporated into their programs to help their clients manage pain, stress, or painful medical conditions. I get resumes from business school graduates, personal assistants, and human resources people who want to know how they can enter this field as well. But that's just the start. The new marijuana economy will need the help of marketers, real estate agents, inventors, attorneys, and accountants. We will see physicians and alternative medicine professionals who will specialize in cannabis-centered care.

Marijuana-based tourism is already flourishing among Colorado's bed and breakfasts, spas, and bus tour companies. Is it so unlikely that wedding planners or caterers will start planning events where marijuana is as freely available to adults as alcohol? Why couldn't gift card and coupon-book companies bring cannabis companies to the attention of wider audiences? Is it outside the range of possibility that universities and technical schools will start offering cannabis horticulture classes?

The marijuana subculture has long embraced the arts. When marijuana is out of the closet, we can expect marijuana-friendly musicians, writers, artists, and performers to be more warmly embraced by the mainstream. Several musicians have already contacted me about doing concerts when our Cannabis Ranch amphitheater opens.

EXPECT TO SEE A SECOND-WAVE "MICROMOVEMENT" WITHIN THE LARGER CANNABIS INDUSTRY

Every year, more small craft breweries go into business and find success, even though the market is seemingly saturated with major beverage companies, such as Budweiser and Coors, and medium-level breweries, such as New Belgium and Sierra Nevada. Local municipalities, eager to boost tax revenues and tourism, allow small entrepreneurs to operate micro- and even nanobreweries.

Once the major players become dominant nationally, the same will happen with cannabis. Small craft growers will focus on some unique feature that they alone can provide—exotic strains, perhaps, or ultra-organic cultivation. We may even see the birth of a local marijuana café culture like the one so prevalent in Amsterdam.

EXPECT TO SEE THE REBIRTH OF INDUSTRIAL HEMP

Industrial hemp, a low-THC cannabis crop, is likely to return as states legalize marijuana. Just as Thomas Jefferson and George Washington were saying two centuries ago, hemp has a wonderful array of uses, from food, to fuel, to fibers. In Europe, I learned that several car manufacturers use hemp-based plastics in the molded door finishes in high-end automobiles because those cars are required by law to be 100 percent recyclable. Ben Dronkers, the owner of Sensi Seeds and my host while in Amsterdam, has been a passionate force in the hemp world for decades. If you buy a high-end BMW or Mercedes in Europe, the door panels are made with his hemp.

As I write this, nearly a thousand acres in Colorado are devoted to hemp production to extract the analgesic cannabidiol (CBD). Other U.S. states are moving forward with legalizing hemp. I expect this area of hemp production to grow first for two reasons: (1) Hemp is naturally low in THC and may encounter less federal resistance when it comes time to ship this product across state lines; (2) CBD is a valuable medical commodity. At this writing, it remains to be seen how the U.S. federal government will react to out-of-state shipments of CBD oil.

Commercial adoption of hemp for textiles, fuels, food, and the like will take longer because the United States is technologically behind other industrialized nations, such as Canada, China, Russia, India, and many in Europe. Sadly, because marijuana has been under attack in the United States since the middle of the nineteenth century, it never really experienced the effects of the Industrial Revolution here. The large-scale machines used to process cotton and other fibers don't work well with hemp. If this country wants to embrace hemp again, it will need to innovate, invent, and build its hemp-processing infrastructure. This is an area of low-hanging opportunity waiting for smart inventors and venture capitalists.

PUBLIC PERCEPTION OF MARIJUANA AND ITS USERS WILL EVOLVE IN KEY AREAS

I don't think it's far off the mark to say that marijuana users today are still regarded as unambitious stoners. Even within the industry, we still use terms like "stoners" and "potheads" to talk about ourselves. When marijuana use is as normal as asking for a glass of wine or stepping out for a cigarette, that perception will change and morph into something more accommodating. Specifically, I see three areas that will generate challenges and change:

Case Law, Due Process, and Workplace Safety Standards

I've already discussed how law enforcement and the judicial system are evolving to the new realities of legal marijuana. As a nation, we will need to hammer out a driving-under-the-influence standard, for example. But on the civil level, I have to wonder what will happen to employment practices when marijuana is no longer considered illegal. I think we can all agree that we don't want a forklift operator to use marijuana on the job. But what about an employee who works from home three days a week and smokes in the privacy of her home because of the debilitating effects of rheumatoid arthritis? I know of one case where an employee with a medical marijuana recommendation from his doctor was fired after he tested positive for THC in a random drug test. The firing was upheld in his suit against his former employers. This is a serious gray area that must be addressed and resolved in the courts.

Substance Abuse Education for Children

As a society, we need to get clear on the new messages we're delivering to our kids about marijuana use. I see no reason why we can't talk about marijuana the way we talk about tobacco and alcohol; all three are not appropriate for kids.

We'll need to educate kids about the developmental risks to their growing bodies posed by those three substances. And we will want to break down for them the relative dangers of each, just as we have in the past. To my mind, it's clear that marijuana poses the lowest risk, but it remains to be seen if parents, educators, and public health officials will take the same view. I know what I'd tell my daughters: Prescription drugs can kill you upon first use. Street drugs such as heroin or meth can addict you. Alcohol can foist upon you an hour of stupidity that you will regret for the rest of your life. Marijuana is the least of these dangers, but you need to be safe and you certainly don't want to be driving under its influence.

Public Health Issues for All of Us

No health organization has ever established a fatal dosage level for marijuana. While I concur that it is virtually impossible to kill your-self with marijuana, and while we can be proud that we're selling a product that is *safer* than, say, alcohol, only a fool would argue that it is *completely safe.*

Only an open enlightened public debate supported by rigorous scientific research will help us determine the scope of marijuana's risks—and benefits. Unfortunately, because marijuana is currently a federally illegal substance, research on its uses and impact is sorely lacking in the United States. I expect that universities in states in which marijuana is legal for medical use will mount fresh studies. Yes, I know that we can point to numerous worldwide studies, but science tends to operate by local (i.e., national) consensus. The more American universities and researchers work with marijuana, the more likely they are to be comfortable with the overall findings.

Does that mean that companies like mine should not be allowed to sell marijuana? I think we should. From tobacco to Ferraris to doughnuts, U.S. culture permits the sale of countless products that are not *completely safe.* Only moderation and prudence can help navi-gate the trade-offs. Personally, I believe the long-standing historic research, which has found that marijuana is relatively harmless com-pared to tobacco, alcohol, sugar, salt, and a host of other drugs or foods. But the industry is constantly developing new products that ought to be investigated properly. For example, there are questions about the risks of vape pens, smokeless devices that allow users to take a hit of THC or nicotine without inhaling the harmful by-products of combustion. But any cannabist who is reasonable and a critical thinker has to be interested in what new research into these devices will find. Will we be using them twenty years from now, or will new devices be invented that are even safer?

Good cannabis education for adults will also teach about the trade-offs inherent in using tinctures and edibles. At first glance, they appear to be the safest way to consume marijuana because you sidestep the issue of smoking altogether. But dosages will continue to be difficult to assess in edibles, and the levels of fats, sugars, and salt in edibles further complicate the issue. What good is it to pass up vape pens because you're concerned about the risk of carcinogens, only to ingest a lot of fattening calories instead?

I predict edibles will become the chief locus of marijuana horror stories. The number of pothead foodies will grow. People will experiment with marijuana in their kitchens, and there will be mistakes. I can see it now: People will have near-hallucinogenic responses after eating commercially prepared or homemade edibles, and the media will blow the stories out of proportion. Antimarijuana activists use this as an excuse to say: See? We never should have made this *drug* legal! My response to that is: No—we need to teach people to read labels and follow the instructions of their budtenders. We don't ban habanero peppers because enthusiastic home chefs get some in their eyes. This is another reason why it would be unwise to move marijuana outside the realm of dispensaries. Trained staffers can best guide customers.

Commercially prepared edibles probably should be manufactured in dedicated facilities. The issue of cross-contamination, already so important in the food allergy community, is equally important with marijuana. And most important, edibles need to be prepared and packaged in such a way that they are not inviting to or accessible by children.

FROM WHERE I STAND, the fact that we can even talk seriously about the new marijuana economy is evidence that the United States is becoming a better society.

For close to a hundred years, the United States put its sons and daughters through hell because they dared to play with a plant that made them feel good. The nation's might, and its spite, was so great that it sucked other nations into that hellish vortex. The American war on drugs hasn't just wreaked misery on Americans—it's crushed and killed human beings all over this planet. Citizens of neighboring countries and far-off continents have died, and are still dying, to serve America's illegal marijuana habit.

A habit that shouldn't be illegal in the first place.

So when reactionary politicians and pundits say legal marijuana is just a charade, I have to shake my head. It's so not. It's about evolving into something better than we once were. It's about moving away from the sins of the past. It's about becoming the best "we" we can be.

Call me crazy, but I feel as if the entire United States is going through a process of enlightenment. That's the theme I see emerging through the eyes of the cannabis industry. The legal marijuana story warms my heart because it reveals an America that is ready to right past wrongs and grow as a society.

I believe it's finally happening.

16

THE CANNABIS RANCH

I LOVE THE SMELL OF WEED IN THE MORNING.

In the wild, the female cannabis plant may not flower until the end of the growing season, when the days grow shorter. But indoors, we can manipulate the lighting to trigger early flowering. In our grows, the young plant is about two weeks into the flower cycle when its buds begin to sprout. Prior to that moment, the plant puts all its efforts into the vegetative growth cycle—producing leaves and growing tall toward the light. Then one day you see the first nubby cluster of small leaves that announces that something different is about to happen, that all these leaves and the race to height has not been for naught. There's a preordained purpose here.

The next time I come into the grow, I know that those nubs have become flowers overnight because that section of the building is suddenly perfumed with the scent of lemons and pine and berries and apples and cinnamon and cloves and honey and mangos and grapes and cherry nectar and spicy mint.

That's when I know that the magic has begun.

The longer I am in this business, the more I am struck by how closely the growth of these plants mirrors that of our own lives. When they start out, the clones look so fragile you can hardly imagine what they can achieve on their own. But every gene in their system is imprinted with the knowledge of how to survive, grow, and thrive. They follow those instructions, and their maturity is marked by the arrival of beautiful, blossoming buds.

People are the same way. Businesses—the good ones, at least— are too.

The plants have taught me so much, more than I ever thought they would when I first chose to become their steward.

I have worked in businesses before that didn't earn their keep by growing living things. I didn't have the opportunity to interact with nature the same way that I do now.

When I was young and foolish, I focused on finding business opportunities, pouncing on them, and wringing every drop of profit from them. Profit was my only goal. What else was there?

Six years later, I'm still a red-blooded American capitalist. Yes, I still believe that starting a business is one of the most rewarding experiences a human can have.

But it's not the only one.

I believe every human being longs to be creative and to watch his or her creativity bear fruit.

Businesspeople are no different. They're just not accustomed to calling what they do *creative*.

That word scares a lot of people in the corporate world.

When young people graduate from the Harvard or Wharton schools of business and enter the workforce, they're told to pay their dues, to follow the rules that have served businesspeople in good stead for hundreds of years. Their path to success, if in fact they even achieve it, is paved with musts.

Things must be done this way . . .

A prudent investor must act this way . . .

A savvy business must move forward in this way . . .

Businesspeople like to brag that they're all about taking risks. But so much of their time is spent minimizing risk. Say that young people followed the musts upon graduation. In six years' time, where would they be? Would they be ready to take over a major corporation? Probably not. If they tried, they'd be laughed out of the office.

You only have six years of experience! What can you possibly know?

Contrast that experience with mine: In six years, I and my fellow ganjapreneurs have invented an industry.

When we started, marijuana wasn't just something corporations didn't do; it was illegal.

The day our product became legal for medical purposes, there were no guidelines, no rules, no musts. Everyone who was paid to govern our industry—from the regulators to the judges—had no idea how to respond. It was still just too new.

What did we do? We got creative.

We went out and started flying by the seats of our pants. When a question cropped up, we answered it. When banks said they couldn't serve us, we moved to others. When those kicked us out, we improvised. When the states and feds demanded their tax money, we figured out ways to pay it. When our crops did poorly, we figured out how to boost our yields.

Three years in, our firm won our industry's top prize.

Five years in, we did it again.

Six years in, we'll gross $20 million in sales.

Twenty years from now, when the cannabis industry is old hat and everyone looks back, they'll see that we were the ones who set the standard. When we started, it was a blank canvas, a block of marble, the silence of a song that had yet to be written. What we do with this opportunity will be guided by our vision, free will, and the decisions we make.

What could be more creative than that?

IN SEPTEMBER 2014, we closed on the 15-acre site that would become the Cannabis Ranch. The long work of making the dream a reality was solidly ahead of us, but I thought of a fun way to mark this milestone. I invited some friends and employees to come out to bless this site on which we would build a dream. Then, on our private land, we loaded a bowl of Ghost Train Haze, the best weed in the world, and had a smoke.

I'd come a long way from the day I snuck a puff of Jake's life-changing weed on the seventeenth hole of the Red Rocks Country Club. The day I tasted what quality marijuana could be like. Our company had taken its baby steps, faltered, fallen, but gotten right back up. Employees had come and gone. I'd bonded with some new mentors, made lots of new friends. And gained a legion of loyal customers.

Now, on the site of a former airplane junkyard, amid this moonscape of dead weeds and cratered soil, we were going to make something beautiful. We were going to heal the land by excising the toxins from its soil. And happily, we had caught a break on the cost of the remediation. I had budgeted $800,000, but it actually would cost closer to $640,000. When the work was done, we'd be left with a giant hole in the ground. We'd use that hole to build a very deep basement level and a sturdy foundation upon which to build the rest of the building.

Ours was going to be some basement: 50,000 square feet, about the size of a football field or a large supermarket. The hole would be excavated to a 14-foot height, allowing us to build a complete indoor grow underground. When we were done, that underground grow would become home to six hundred grow lights—a far cry from the sixteen lights I'd installed in my first grow back in 2009.

Remember my rule of thumb: More lights equals more weed.

The Cannabis Ranch construction called for a second grow facility just next door: a 100,000-square-foot greenhouse, double the size of the indoor grow. All together, we'd have 150,000 square feet of growing space to start.

Now, admittedly, the greenhouse still represented a leap of faith on our part. We would be growing in part by the light of the sun for the first time ever. We would still need grow lights to make up for the seasonal nature of sunlight. We were studying different options, trying to decide which lights would be best for us. It wasn't a complex problem, because people have been growing fruits and vegetables in greenhouses for years. But this would be the first such facility for marijuana in the world.

Yes, I still needed about another $16 million to take the project to completion—the visitor center on top of the basement grow, the restaurant, and the amphitheater. But I wasn't worried. I was locked in the eternal dance with investors. I already had $9 million from two institutional investors. Being able to mention such investors to would-be backers would give the newcomers confidence.

If people asked me why I wasn't terribly concerned about finding investors for the remainder of the project, I'd point to the model of the Cannabis Ranch I had kept in my office for the last year and a half, and I'd tell them of the vision I saw so long ago.

I was confident that the Cannabis Ranch would ensure that Green Man Cannabis would become the largest legal marijuana company in the world. All told, when the two facilities were finished, we'd have the equivalent of three football fields in which to grow marijuana. I projected that we'd be growing 55,000 pounds of marijuana—or 27 *tons*—a year.

Once I turned on the lights in those grows, I would be kick-starting the economic engine. From that moment on, investors would be nice, but if they took a while to emerge, we'd be fine. The plants in those grows would be fully capable of paying their own way.

The Cannabis Ranch's progress signaled a shift in our company's future, one that mandated a new direction for me. We were now running not one but two companies. One grew and sold marijuana. The other raised capital and created business development opportunities for Green Man to grow. One company was about ensuring an even supply of product and making customers happy when they walked in the door to buy weed. The other was concerned with ensuring the growth of the Green Man brand. The latter is the bigger deal.

Potentially, there was a conflict of interest there. When I first started down the path toward building the Cannabis Ranch, I knew that such a dilemma eventually would arise. Going forward, the Cannabis Ranch would function as the landlord to Green Man Cannabis. I wanted what was best for both companies, but it was conceivable that, in the future, what was best for the Green Man might not be the best for the Cannabis Ranch, and vice versa.

My course had always been clear: In the coming months, I would have to resign as CEO of the marijuana operating company to take the helm at the new company, American Cannabis Partners. I would continue to drive the vision and business development and stay on as the chairman of the board to both companies, but I would not manage Green Man's day-to-day operations.

So now I was presiding over what I thought was yet another first: the first executive search for the CEO of a legal marijuana company. We were putting out feelers to locate a top-level corporate brain, a Harvard MBA type, to take the company into the next decade and beyond. We had attracted institutional investors; now we needed great management. I didn't think it would be hard to find the right person. Lately I had met so many professionals who were eager to do something, anything, in the world of marijuana. Was it so unrealistic to think that the right CEO was somewhere out there?

Everywhere I looked, I faced bittersweet decisions. I loved Green Man. Moving into a new role would be hard, but it would be the best way to grow Green Man to its full potential.

It would also allow me to look at big-picture issues, such as the overall perception of the industry, which I had begun thinking of on a regular basis.

Every year one of my daughters' schools has a silent auction to raise money for school events and trips throughout the year. Each year I offered the parent-teacher organization a coupon good for up to twenty adults to tour my grow facilities. I know the demand is there, because experience has shown me that people are insatiably curious about the burgeoning marijuana business. So far the school has rejected my donation each year. My pride isn't wounded, you understand. But as the years go by, and I make a point of offering every year, my gesture has become more about gauging how receptive the school is to my offer than anything else.

The struggle going forward is about normalizing marijuana. It's about making it part of our cultural landscape again, as okay as every liquor store you pass to and from work every day.

The Cannabis Ranch is my chance to normalize marijuana, to bring it to the world on such a scale that it cannot be ignored. The way tourists will progress through the Cannabis Ranch is fraught with symbolism. They'll descend from the reception hall of the visitors' center into the basement grow. From there, they'll walk down a glass-walled hallway, beholding the fragrant jungle coming to life under the lights.

On the far end of the basement grow, they'll come to a set of doors that will lead them to a bank of elevators. After entering, the elevators will rise, and when the doors open, our visitors will be standing in our glass-enclosed greenhouse. Right in the middle of the action.

I said before that I am not an artist, not a poet, not a creative person in the artistic sense. But I cannot ignore the power of a beautiful metaphor. Our visitors will be embarking on a journey that mimics America's own journey of enlightenment. As they move from the basement, they're leaving marijuana's past behind. When they enter the greenhouse, they'll be looking at the future. From the closet out into the open. From the darkness into the light.

It doesn't get clearer than that.

AT THE BEGINNING OF THIS STORY, I told you that I was searching for something. That I needed this business to succeed not because I craved the money but because it might teach me the way to joy and love. Today I know I've found it. I have never known as much happiness as I have growing and selling this gorgeous plant. It's been the most wonderful business endeavor of my life.

When I look at myself in the mirror, I know I'm not the same man who nearly destroyed his health running a business into the ground. Yes, I'm older. Yes, I've fallen down. But I've gotten back up and chosen to push ahead. And despite any obstacles and resistance and betrayal, I have not just survived but thrived.

I'm not ashamed to say that marijuana has been my salvation. And in a larger sense, I think marijuana legalization ultimately will be recognized as one of the salvational stories of the United States.

I can see how the business has touched others in my personal life.

My daughters are growing up absorbing the lesson that their father is following his bliss and creating something that is meaningful to others as well.

My mom is watching her son achieve a dream. Her golden years are also graced with the memory of her late partner, who was touched by the plant before his passing.

My father, the physician, has been blessed with a new educational experience late in life. Recently, when he was diagnosed with Parkinson's disease, he began experimenting with marijuana-derived cannibidiol as a way to treat his condition. He noticed marked improvement in controlling aspects of the disease. As a doctor, he couldn't resist sharing what he'd learned with others. I was proud to watch as he enthusiastically wrote up his findings and presented them at a medical conference.

Corey, the grower who did so much to make our business a success, has taken my advice and begun consulting with up-and-coming marijuana businesses throughout the country. I know this will be the start of a long and profitable career for him. Proving my point that you must always look for the win-win, I'm pleased to say we will be sharing in that success together.

My friend and real estate broker Dax recently got involved in the industry, developing an app called Green Spott that allows customers to order online through a smartphone.

Most important, millions of people—Americans and non-Americans—who might have been jailed or killed or otherwise targeted by the war on marijuana will instead have the opportunity to lead positive, fulfilling lives.

Many others, millions perhaps, will find their joy and their next career in this business. Maybe you will too. If you're the slightest bit curious, you owe it to yourself to do the due diligence.

Tell you what: Someday soon, the first generation of our plants will be settling into life at the Green Man Cannabis Ranch. The ones under glass will be our first to see what a Colorado spring or summer is like. The first to feel the rays of the sun on their leaves. They don't have to hide anymore, and neither do we.

The next time you're in Denver, I'd welcome the chance to introduce you to our world. Book a long layover. The Green Man Cannabis Ranch will be waiting. I invite you to stop by and say *high*.

ACKNOWLEDGMENTS

IT'S NOT OFTEN THAT AN ENTREPRENEUR GETS A CHANCE to write a book about a fascinating new growth industry that has changed his life. By any measure, I know I'm a lucky man, but I would not have been able to create the book you hold in your hands without the help, motivation, and support of a great number of people. Every one of them deserve a thank-you from a grateful author and friend.

John Zakhem, you're a good attorney, good golfer, and a great friend.

This book began as the spark of an idea mentioned to my literary agent, Yfat Reiss Gendell, who recognized the potential, helped me develop the concept, and found *Big Weed* a good cowriter and home. For this I am indebted to Yfat and her entire team at Foundry Literary + Media. I'm lucky I landed in your stable of authors.

Joseph D'Agnese, Yfat brought us together, and it has worked wonderfully. You have been a competent and calming influence as I moved through the great unknown of writing my first book. I appreciate your professionalism and the outstanding quality of your work. I have enjoyed working with you.

My editor, Emily Carleton, and her executive editor, Elisabeth Dyssegaard, at Palgrave Macmillan pounced on this little book and embraced it passionately. Their entire team, who fearlessly volunteered for a "research trip" to the wilds of Colorado, is responsible for bringing this book to the rest of the world.

To everyone at Green Man Cannabis, you know who you are, but especially: Barb Visher—your personal and professional support has inspired me, enabled me and encouraged me through the many ups and downs over the past five years. To my founding partners, Gary Schwartz, Audra and Scott Richmond, and Mike Visher: So many of the stories in this book are your stories, too. To our longtime employees, Kristin Aichinger, Jen Schmidt, Dustin, Zach, Dane, Sam, Hillary, Holly, and more: Your dedication and care is appreciated beyond words. This company could not be what it is today without your faith and determination. Corey—I mean every word: You are the best among the best.

In a rapidly changing business, you come to rely on the advice of a trusted few. In this regard I am grateful for the advice of Christian Sederberg and Ed Rosenthal.

I could never have gotten this business off the ground without the encouragement, intelligent counsel, and support of Mr. Pink— you are a prince among men and one of the most astute businessmen I know. And no, you cannot be Mr. Black or pick your own name.

And to Dax Gurgan—you are my brother from a different mother.

My life could not be complete without the ones I love. I'm grateful, Dad, that you were here for part of this journey. Mom, without your support I would feel lacking. Thanks too to my brother, John.

To my wonderful daughters, Hannah, Harper, and Hadley (HaHaHa), I am inspired by the love I feel for each of you. I am proud of the people you are and I enjoy your company—I love you each with all my heart.

And Rebecca: You are light and love, a true earth angel, nearly as beautiful on the outside as you are on the inside. You are the personification of loving kindness, loving beyond expectation or reason, inspiring, comforting, and supportive. God gave superpowers to the right human being. The benefit of your readings, channelings, and intuitive insight have given me authentic faith. I acknowledge this wouldn't have been possible without you for a number of reasons, not the least of which because you introduced me to Yfat. Last, and in no way the least, thank you for agreeing to marry me.

NOTES

INTRODUCTION

Details about how Colorado used its medical marijuana fund to prop up its state budget was drawn from an article by Tim Hoover, "Ritter Turns to Medical-Marijuana Fund to Help Balance Colorado Budget," *Denver Post*, August 24, 2010.

Admittedly, the history of the U.S. Prohibition era of alcohol is not a perfect analog to marijuana prohibition, but it's one that is mined often by marijuana activists seeking lessons from that history. I found the best discussion in the book *Marijuana Is Safer: So Why Are We Driving People to Drink?* by Steve Fox, Paul Armentano, and Mason Tvert (White River Junction, VT: Chelsea Green, updated and expanded edition, 2013).

1. BRAVE NEW WORLD

The six qualifying conditions for medical marijuana in Colorado are cancer, HIV/ AIDS, glaucoma, and conditions causing one or more of the following: severe pain, cachexia (wasting syndrome), severe nausea, seizures, or persistent muscle spasms. The Marijuana Policy Project, an advocacy group, summarizes the United States's medical marijuana laws and patient rights and protections in a PDF available at the URL: http://www.mpp.org/assets/pdfs/library/MMJLawsSummary.pdf

2. MY EDUCATION

The distinctions between the various species of cannabis are discussed in *Ed Rosenthal's Marijuana Grower's Handbook* by Ed Rosenthal (Oakland, CA: Quick American, 2010).

Throughout this book, my "tasting notes" on various marijuana strains are based on my own experiences with those strains. A more comprehensive list of strains and their attributes can be found at Leafly.com.

Discussions of human interaction with the cannabis plant in ancient history are drawn largely from *The Pot Book: A Complete Guide to Cannabis, Its Role in Medicine, Politics, Science, and Culture,* edited by Julie Holland, MD (Rochester, VT: Park Street Press, 2010). See, in particular, chapter 2, "Early/Ancient History," by Chris Bennett, and chapter 4, "The Botany of Cannabis," by Lyle E. Craker, PhD, and Zoe Gardner.

The discussion of U.S. history and politics in the nineteenth and twentieth centuries with respect to cannabis is drawn chiefly from *Marijuana Is Safer: So Why Are We Driving People to Drink?* by Steve Fox, Paul Armentano, and Mason Tvert (White River Junction, VT: Chelsea Green, updated and expanded edition, 2013);

Ed Rosenthal's Marijuana Grower's Handbook, and *The Pot Book,* edited by Holland, particularly chapter 3, "Recent History," by David Malmo-Levine.

The discovery of cannabis- and cocaine-tainted pipes in Shakespeare's garden was reported in "Bard 'Used Drugs for Inspiration,'" BBC News, March 1, 2001 (http://news.bbc.co.uk/2/hi/entertainment/1195939.stm) and "Drugs Clue to Shakespeare's Genius," CNN.com, March 1, 2001 (http://edition.cnn.com/2001/WORLD/europe/UK/03/01/shakespeare.cannabis). Those news reports were based on this scientific paper: J. F. Thackeray, N. J. Van Der Merwe, and T. A. Van Der Merwe, "Chemical Analysis of Residues from Seventeenth-Century Clay Pipes from Stratford-upon-Avon and Environs," *South African Journal of Science* 97 (2001): 19–21.

Quotes from Thomas Jefferson, George Washington, and John Adams can be found in *The Pot Book* by Holland. Monticello, the Jefferson residence historic site, offers an extensive, fascinating list of hemp references drawn from the writings of Jefferson: (http://www.monticello.org/site/plantation-and-slavery/hemp).

The THC level in cannabis typically is tested and reported each year following competitions in the United States and the Netherlands. The data, frankly, vary according to the labs performing the tests, sampling methods, growing techniques, and types of samples submitted. One gauge is the annual "Earth's Strongest Strains" report published by *High Times* magazine. The 2014 report (http://www.hightimes.com/read/earths-strongest-strains-2014) includes my firm's own SkunkBerry strain. In the 2014 review, *High Times* noted that THC content had risen enough across the board that it could now report several strains at 23 percent or higher, up from a previous level of 20 percent.

The average THC content of cannabis found in Dutch coffee shops was reported in "Dutch Cannabis No Longer So Strong," Netherlands Info Service News Bulletin, June 27, 2013: http://www.nisnews.nl/adb.html, based on a study by the Trimbos Institute commissioned by the Dutch health ministry. In 2011, after a survey by Trimbos found that cannabis sold in shops averaged THC content between 16 and 18 percent, the nation acted to ban cannabis that tested higher than 15 percent.

Details of the collectible market for cannabis-labeled medicine bottles was drawn from antiquecannabisbook.com. A complete collection of all editions of the *United States Pharmacopoeia,* the "cookbook" that taught pharmacists how to prepare various medicinal formulations, that reference cannabis—and the 1942 edition that did not—may be inspected online: http://antiquecannabisbook.com/Appendix/Appendix C.htm.

There's no definitive cut of the film known today as *Reefer Madness,* but you can watch one version for free online: https://archive.org/details/ReeferMadness_479. Likewise, a version of *Hemp for Victory* may be viewed free online: https://archive.org/details/HempForVictoryfixedVersion512kbMp4.

The complete schedules for controlled substance may be found at the U.S. Department of Justice website: http://www.deadiversion.usdoj.gov/21cfr/cfr/2108cfrt.htm. A quick summary of the schedules may be found at: http://www.deadiversion.usdoj.gov/schedules/.

The complete text of the Report of the National Commission on Marihuana and Drug Abuse, 1972, also known as the Shafer Commission, may be found online: http://www.druglibrary.org/schaffer/Library/studies/nc/ncmenu.htm.

Details on the gateway hypothesis are drawn from *Marijuana Is Safer:* by Fox et al. The background on Rockefeller, Mellon, and Hearst's role in demonizing and eradicating cannabis is discussed in chapter 3, "Recent History," by Malmo-Levine, in *The Pot Book,* edited by Holland.

3. FIRST GROW, FIRST BLOOD

I am by no means an expert on cannabis cultivation, but my notes on the plant's growing requirements—humidity and temperatures—is based on personal experience and on *Ed Rosenthal's Marijuana Grower's Handbook* by Ed Rosenthal (Oakland, CA: Quick American, 2010).

4. THE BEAUTY OF FAILURE

Considering the role SkunkBerry has played in my firm's success, I should mention that it is a sativa/indica hybrid. You can find further reviews online: http://theweed snobs.com/skunk-berry-review/ and http://marijuana.com/community/threads/skunk berry-marijuana-strain-review.309550/. Jack Herer is another hybrid (http://www .leafly.com/sativa/jack-herer) bred by Sensi Seeds. Learn more about the late activist Herer online: http://www.jackherer.com.

5. DON'T BANK ON IT

The banking dilemma facing legal cannabis companies has been covered by prominent U.S. news organizations. A sampling of the best articles must include: "Banks Say No to Marijuana Money, Legal or Not" by Serge F. Kovaleski, *New York Times,* January 11, 2014: http://www.nytimes.com/2014/01/12/us/banks-say-no-to-marijuana-money-le gal-or-not.html; "Pot's Money Problem" by Alex Altman, *Time,* January 27, 2014, pp. 32–35; and "Pot Businesses Allowed to Open Accounts with US Banks" by Alison Ve-kshin, Bloomberg: http://www.bloomberg.com/news/2014-02-14/treasury-lets-banks -offer-accounts-to-pot-businesses.html. I should add that the headline of the last article proved overly optimistic; banks are still waiting for action from Congress before granting cannabis firms access to banking accounts.

As proof that the all-cash position of cannabis firms is untenable and dangerous, the *Time* article detailed the July 2013 murders in Bakersfield, California, of a medical marijuana dispensary owner and a security guard and the October 2012 kidnapping and brutalization of another dispensary owner in Orange County, California.

The number of Mexicans killed in recent years in drug violence and the details about the $206 million cash seizure, the largest in history, comes from "Cocaine Un-limited: How a Mexican Drug Cartel Makes Its Billions" by Patrick Radden Keefe, *New York Times Magazine,* June 15, 2012: http://www.nytimes.com/2012/06/17 /magazine/how-a-mexican-drug-cartel-makes-its-billions.html. Details of the $15 million seizure comes from "Inside the Incredible Booming Subterranean Marijuana Railroad," a fascinating look at the underground tunnels used by drug lords to smuggle marijuana into the United States and cash out, by Jason Kersten, *GQ* magazine (January 2014): http://www.gq.com/news-politics/newsmakers/201401/marijuana-ra ilroad-mexican-drug-cartel-tunnels.

6. THE HAZE OF PARANOIA

The official website of the state of Colorado's Medical Marijuana Enforcement Division is: http://www.colorado.gov/cs/Satellite/Rev-MMJ/CBON/1251581331216.

The Ronald Reagan Presidential Foundation and Library regards the Just Say No program as one of the hallmarks of First Lady Nancy Reagan's legacy: http://www .reaganfoundation.org/details_t.aspx?p=RR1005NRL&lm=reagan&args_a=cms

&args_b=10&argsb–N&tx=1203. An article that offers a contrary view is "Why Just Say No Doesn't Work" by Scott O. Lilienfeld and Hal Arkowitz, *Scientific American,* December 19, 2013: http://www.scientificamerican.com/article/why-just-say-no-does nt-work. Another article, "Whatever Happened to 'Just Say No'?" by Mark Stricherz, *The Atlantic,* April 29, 2014 (http://www.theatlantic.com/politics/archive/2014/04 /ghost-of-just-say-no/361322) argues that the decline of the program is due in part to the success of medical marijuana programs and the "'very substantial increase in the number of adults who use marijuana daily or near daily' . . . the share of adults who have tried pot has risen to 38 percent from 24 percent in 1977."

The official website of the Drug Abuse Resistance Education (D.A.R.E.) program is http://www.dare.org. In his article "Drug Abuse Resistance Education: The Effectiveness of DARE," the sociologist David J. Hanson writes: "Scientific evaluation studies have consistently shown that DARE is ineffective in reducing the use of alcohol and drugs and is sometimes even counterproductive—worse than doing nothing. That's the conclusion of the U.S. General Accounting Office, the U.S. Surgeon General, the National Academy of Sciences, and the U.S. Department of Education, among many others" (via http://www.alcoholfacts.org/DARE.html). For a more comprehensive look at the scientific literature, see Google Scholar's listing of articles on the efficacy of the program: http://scholar.google.com/scholar?q=efficacy+of+dare +program&btnG=&hl=en&as_sdt=0%2C34&as_vis=1.

My continuing observations on the history of marijuana prohibition in the United States, the impact of harsh penalties, and the benefits to the judicial system at large when millions of individuals are arrested and thrust through the system are drawn primarily from personal experience, *Marijuana Is Safer: So Why Are We Driving People to Drink?* by Steve Fox, Paul Armentano, and Mason Tvert (White River Junction, VT: Chelsea Green, updated and expanded edition, 2013); and *The Pot Book: A Complete Guide to Cannabis, Its Role in Medicine, Politics, Science, and Culture,* edited by Julie Holland, MD (Rochester, VT: Park Street Press, 2010), particularly chapter 3, "Recent History," by David Malmo-Levine. Eric Schlosser's assertion that penalties for marijuana can be stiffer than those for murder in some U.S. states is found in his lengthy essay on marijuana in his book, *Reefer Madness: Sex, Drugs, and Cheap Labor in the American Black Market* (New York: Houghton Mifflin, 2013).

7. SEED TO SALE TO BUST

For a look at the modern RFID tagging technology implemented to ensure seed-to-sale integrity, please see "RFID Tag Track Marijuana from Seed to Sale in Colorado" by Rebecca Hiscott, *Mashable,* February 11, 2014 (http://mashable.com/2014/02/11 /marijuana-rfid-tracking). Some marijuana advocates oppose the seed-to-sale system, arguing that its ultimate steps invade patient confidentiality, as discussed in "Medical Marijuana Seed-to-Sale Tracking System Already Worrying Advocates—but Should It?" by Michael Roberts, *Westword,* October 21, 2011 (http://blogs.westword.com /latestword/2011/10/medical_marijuana_seed_to_sale.php).

8. THE CANNABIS RANCH

A photo of the aircraft graveyard in its heyday was posted by a third party to the photo-sharing website Flickr: https://www.flickr.com/photos/rlunde/6331214648/. Readers may view recent photos of the site posted by my company at greenmancannabisranch .com.

9. FAMILY: HAGESETH; GENUS: *CANNABIS*

My discussion of adolescent use of marijuana is informed by my personal experience as a parent and by details provided in numerous books and articles over the years. Frankly, the *physiological* arguments for why young people should avoid marijuana are equivocal. In the text *Marijuana Is Safer: So Why Are We Driving People to Drink?* by Steve Fox, Paul Armentano, and Mason Tvert (White River Junction, VT: Chelsea Green, updated and expanded edition, 2013), particularly their discussion in chapter 3, "Removing the 'Toxic' from Intoxication: An Objective Comparison of the Effects of Alcohol and Marijuana," the authors summarize the science behind physiological impacts thusly: "Adolescents should also be advised to avoid cannabis, as it remains unclear whether marijuana, like alcohol, adversely affects the developing brain" (p. 38). A Duke University study, "Persistent Cannabis Users Show Neuropsychological Decline from Childhood to Midlife," by Madeline H. Meier et al., published in the *Proceedings of the National Academy of Sciences of the United States of America,* Vol. 109, no. 40, E2657-E2664, October 2, 2012, (http://www.pnas.org/content/109/40/E2657. abstract?sid=7a2a7f1f-ca77-40c4-8970-c758ca07561d), received a good deal of attention when it was used to bolster an antimarijuana campaign in Colorado: "Colorado Tries Hard to Convince Teens That Pot is Bad for You," by Maanvi Singh, NPR, September 17, 2014 (http://www.npr.org/blogs/health/2014/09/17/348997416/colorado -tries-hard-to-convince-teens-that-pots-bad-for-you), but even the resulting public service announcement had to admit that the results of the study were disputed by a subsequent study, "Correlations between Cannabis Use and IQ Change in the Dunedin Cohort Are Consistent with Confounding from Socioeconomic Status," by Ole Rogeberg, *Proceedings of the National Academy of Sciences of the United States of America* Vol. 11, no. 110, 4251-4254, March 12, 2013 (http://www.pnas.org/content/110/11/4251) which examined the same data. More recent studies have centered upon whether marijuana with higher THC levels will have a stronger impact upon young brains. One article that investigated this issue is "This is Your Brain on Drugs," by Abigail Sullivan Moore, *New York Times,* October 29, 2014 (http://www.nytimes.com/2014/11/02 /education/edlife/this-is-your-brain-on-drugs-marijuana-adults-teens.html).

Unfortunately, adolescents who use marijuana are likely to suffer other consequences that are far clearer and are more compelling reasons for avoiding the substance: In current U.S. society, young people who are caught using marijuana tend to pay a higher price than those who use alcohol, namely: a criminal record, loss of education and employment opportunities. Young people are still developing their understanding of moderation, and are liable to overindulge, which can lead to driving under the influence. They are unlikely to use any technology, such as vaporizers, to reduce their risks from combustion and are thus at risk for pulmonary damage. Last, adolescent usage of street drugs is always alarming because it is virtually impossible to know what drugs bought off the street actually contain.

One of the best discussions on marijuana I've found for parents is authored by medical sociologist and drug abuse expert Marsha Rosenbaum; in *The Pot Book: A Complete Guide to Cannabis, Its Role in Medicine, Politics, Science, and Culture,* edited by Julie Holland, MD (Rochester, VT: Park Street Press, 2010), chapter 30, titled "What to Tell the Children," contains a brief summary of Rosenbaum's work. The full text of her pamphlet, titled "Safety First: A Reality-Based Approach to Teens and Drugs" and distributed by the Drug Policy Alliance, is mandatory reading for all parents and can be found online: http://www.drugpolicy.org/sites/default/files /DPA_SafetyFirst_2014.pdf.

In 2013, CNN's medical correspondent Dr. Sanjay Gupta, a neurosurgeon by training, made a very public about-face on the issue of medical marijuana, resulting in two documentaries, which can be found online: *Weed* (https://www.youtube .com/watch?v=Dn9eTC1mNTk) and *Weed 2* (https://www.youtube.com/watch?v=tA Fu-Ihwyzg).

A fine resource for parents and others investigating the potential of cannabidiol (CBD) for family members suffering from seizures and other ailments is the website of the nonprofit organization Project CBD (http://www.projectcbd.org). Whether farmers who are growing hemp will be able to ship the nonintoxicating CBD oil made from this strain of cannabis out of state is a matter of speculation at this writing. The issue was summarized nicely in "Bid to Expand Medical Marijuana Business Faces Federal Hurdles" by Dave Philipps, *New York Times,* August 23, 2014 (http://www .nytimes.com/2014/08/24/us/bid-to-expand-medical-marijuana-business-faces -federal-hurdles.html).

The impact of cannabis on disease has been documented by a host of different researchers around the world. A 2009 landmark article in the *Journal of Opioid Management,* by University of Washington researcher Sunil Aggarwal and his colleagues surveyed thirty-three U.S.-controlled trial studies published between 1971 and 2009 that reveal cannabis as "safe, effective medicine for specific medical conditions." The full article is behind a paywall at the journal, but the National Institutes of Health stores the article abstract online: http://www.ncbi.nlm.nih.gov/pubmed/19662925, and the Marijuana Policy Project, an advocacy group, posted a press releases on the report and its findings: http://www.mpp.org/states/washington/press-releases/33-us -clinical-studies-show.html. If thirty-three controlled trials are not convincing enough, readers may wish to review a seventy-page report issued by NORML, "Emerging Clinical Application for Cannabis and Cannabinoids: A Review of the Recent Scientific Literature, Sixth Edition," that lists the more than two hundred recent studies dating from 2000 to 2013 that investigated the use and safety of cannabis to treat twenty different conditions. The full report is available online: http://norml.org/pdf_files /NORML_Clinical_Applications_for_Cannabis_and_Cannabinoids.pdf.

More germane to my discussion of cannabis and its impact on cancer patients such as Bob, readers will find part 3, "The Clinical Use of Cannabis," in Holland's *The Pot Book* to be a more manageable read. The introduction, in particular pages 242 to 246, discusses the ability of cannabis to treat the Big Six side effects associated with conventional cancer treatment: depression, anxiety, insomnia, loss of appetite, nausea, and pain. This section of the text explores the U.S. government's obstruction of cannabis research; its "pot farm" in Oxford, Mississippi; the plant's potential use in psychiatry; and more. In the same text I refer readers to chapter 6, "The Endocannabinoid System," by Gregory L. Gerdeman, PhD, and Jason B. Schechter, PhD; and chapter 7, "Anandamide and More," by Raphael Mechoulam, PhD, and Lumír Hanuš.

A compelling documentary, *Clearing the Smoke: The Science of Cannabis,* produced by PBS Montana, investigates the science behind endocannabinoids and can be viewed online: https://www.youtube.com/watch?v=8aTbnO9I-TU.

The full text of the U.S. government's patent #6630507, "Cannabinoids as Antioxidants and Neuroprotectants," can be found online: http://www.google.com /patents/US6630507.

Some examples of old-time advertisements for hasheesh candy and a discussion of its properties can be viewed online: http://www.cannabisculture.com/content/2013 /02/07/Incredible-Delectable-Miracle-19th-Century-Medicine-Hasheesh-Candy.

The "pot brownie" story has been somewhat distorted over time. Alice B. Toklas was the longtime companion of the writer Gertrude Stein. Technically, the recipe was not Toklas's but that of an artist friend named Brion Gysin, who called it "Haschich Fudge." The original recipe can be found online (http://www.brainpickings.org /2013/03/04/the-alice-b-toklas-cookbook-folio-natacha-ledwidge/) and in the 2010 paperback of the cookbook by Harper Perennial.

The controversy over edibles was ratcheted significantly in summer 2014 after Maureen Dowd, a columnist with the *New York Times,* reported having a dysphoric experience after consuming a marijuana-laced chocolate bar on a research trip to Denver. After her column about the experience (http://www.nytimes.com/2014/06/04/opinion /dowd-dont-harsh-our-mellow-dude.html) went viral, reporters in Denver ferreted out that Dowd had been warned about how to consume the product (http://www.the cannabist.co/2014/06/04/was-maureen-dowd-warned-about-edible-marijuana/13113). Dowd noted in that same column that she knew that the candy bar was intended to provide sixteen individual doses, but that information was not indicated on the packaging.

10. BEST IN SHOW

Details on our various winning strains maybe be found online: Super Lemon Haze (http://www.leafly.com/hybrid/super-lemon-haze), the Hells Angels strain (http:// www.leafly.com/hybrid/hells-angel-og), and Jack Herer (http://www.leafly.com/sativa /jack-herer). A discussion of the cannabis plant's origins in the Hindu-Kush ranges of the Himalaya foothills is documented in chapter 1 of *Ed Rosenthal's Marijuana Grower's Handbook* by Ed Rosenthal (Oakland, CA: Quick American, 2010).

The article "Despite Outlaw Image, Hells Angels Sue Often," by Serge F. Kovaleski, *New York Times,* November 28, 2013 (http://www.nytimes.com/2013/11/29/u s/despite-outlaw-image-hells-angels-sue-often.html) may shed light on my encounter with members.

Trichomes are discussed prominently in the Rosenthal text, particularly in part 4, as an indicator of harvesting readiness.

My understanding of the nonuniform nature of cannabis tolerance was informed, in part, by the discussion in *The Pot Book: A Complete Guide to Cannabis, Its Role in Medicine, Politics, Science, and Culture,* edited by Julie Holland, MD (Rochester, VT: Park Street Press, 2010), particularly chapter 12, "Cannabis and Cognition," by Caroline B. Marvin and Carl L. Hart, PhD.

Details of future Cannabis Cups may be found at: http://www.cannabiscup.com.

See the article "420 Meaning: The True Story of How April 20 Became 'Weed Day,'" by Ryan Grim, *Huffington Post,* updated April 19, 2013 (http://www.huffington post.com/2010/04/20/420-meaning-the-true-stor_n_543854.html) which is extensive investigation into the San Rafael, California, story and shares interviews with the original participants.

The H. P. Lovecraft short story often cited as the inspiration for 420 is entitled "In the Walls of Eryx" and is available to read for free at the following URL: http:// www.hplovecraft.com/writings/texts/fiction/iwe.aspx.

11. MARIJUANA'S MECCA

See part I of *Ed Rosenthal's Marijuana Grower's Handbook* by Ed Rosenthal (Oakland, CA: Quick American, 2010), particularly pages 21 to 33, for a discussion of terpenes.

The two seed companies mentioned in this chapter are Sensi Seeds (http:// sensiseeds.com) and Soma Seeds (http://somaseeds.nl). Numerous videos of Soma discussing recipes and other topics can be found at his YouTube channel: https://www .youtube.com/user/somamissionTV.

The story of Rosenthal's ordeal is told in the article "Medical Marijuana Clash Put a Grower in Court" by Dean E. Murphy, *New York Times,* January 21, 2003 (http://www.nytimes.com/2003/01/21/national/21POT.html).

The two Amsterdam cafés mentioned in this chapter are Grey Area (http://www.greyarea.nl) and Green House Seeds (http://greenhouseseeds.nl).

Find the Hash Marihuana & Hemp Museum online at: http://hashmuseum.com.

Articles and photos of the Cannabis Culture Awards I attended may be found at: http://cannabiscultureawards.com/awards/cannabis-culture-awards-2013-amsterdam.

12. MARIJUANA ON THE BALLOT

The complete text of Amendment 64 may be found at: http://www.fcgov.com/mmj/pdf/amendment64.pdf.

The three advocacy groups mentioned in this chapter are the Marijuana Policy Project (http://www.mpp.org), SAFER (http://archive.saferchoice.org), and NORML (http://norml.org). The law firm Vicente Sederberg LLC can be found at: themarijuanalawfirm.com.

The rationale and execution of the "safer than alcohol" campaign is discussed in greater detail in chapter 11, "The Wall Comes Down: Colorado Makes Marijuana Legal," in *Marijuana Is Safer: So Why Are We Driving People to Drink?* by Steve Fox, Paul Armentano, and Mason Tvert (White River Junction, VT: Chelsea Green, updated and expanded edition, 2013).

The issues surrounding marijuana DUIs are summarized in "Driving Under the Influence, of Marijuana" by Maggie Koerth-Baker, *New York Times,* February 17, 2014 (http://www.nytimes.com/2014/02/18/health/driving-under-the-influence-of-marijuana.html). Another interesting report, "Marijuana Case Filings Plummet in Colorado Following Legalization," by John Ingold, *Denver Post,* January 12, 2014, (http://www.denverpost.com/marijuana/ci_24894248/marijuana-case-filings-plummet-colorado-following-legalization), found that even in the period of time from the referendum until the law officially took effect, the number of marijuana arrests declined sharply, which indicates that police and prosecutors pursued fewer cases as a buildup to legalization.

13. LOOKING FOR THE WIN-WIN

Notes regarding the outdoor event were drawn from articles such as "Denver 4/20 rally Draws Mellow Crowd; Police Issue Dozens of Citations" by John Ingold, Matt Miller, and Kate Gibbons, *Denver Post,* April 20, 2014 (http://www.denverpost.com/news/ci_25603926/2014-420-rally-denver-day-2); "Police Hold 22 People at Mass Cannabis Rally in Denver" by Nick Allen, (London) *Daily Telegraph,* April 21, 2014 (http://www.telegraph.co.uk/news/worldnews/northamerica/usa/10777675/Police-hold-22-people-at-mass-cannabis-rally-in-Denver.html); and "With Sales Now Legal, Cannabis Lovers Take Denver's 420 Weekend to New Highs" by Jessica Ravitz, *CNN,* April 21, 2014 (http://www.cnn.com/2014/04/20/us/denver-420-weekend).

Learn more about Ghost Train Haze at http://www.leafly.com/sativa/ghost-train-haze. Details about Breeder Rare Dankness may be found at: http://raredankness.com.

The *CBS This Morning* clip documenting our win can be found at: http://www.cbsnews.com/videos/cannabis-cup-celebrates-all-things-marijuana-on-420-day.

14. INVESTORS

Pegging the exact revenue of the illicit drug trade is virtually impossible, and it's highly frustrating to see various agencies—from U.S. law enforcement to top drug commissions with the United Nations—bandy about figures that might well be meaningless. A 2005 UN World Drug Report (https://www.unodc.org/unodc/en /data-and-analysis/WDR-2005.html) argued that the worldwide illicit drug market produced revenues of $320 billion annually, the worldwide marijuana market gener- ated revenues of $141.80 billion annually, and the U.S. market alone generated half of this latter figure, about $64 billion. A 2013 report issued by the Inter-American Drug Abuse Control Commission of the Organization of American States (available at: http:// www.cicad.oas.org/drogas/elinforme/informeDrogas2013/laEconomicaNarco trafico_ENG.pdf) repeated these estimates but cautioned that numerous experts re- gard them as "implausibly high." Using another methodology, the report continued, the U.S. Office of National Drug Control Policy estimated that in 2012 the total illegal U.S. marijuana market was only between $15 to $30 billion. Government ac- ceptance typically has settled around this range. A 2012 White House report, "What America's Users Spend on Illegal Drugs," pegged the size of the illegal trade in the big four illegal drugs (cocaine, heroin, methamphetamine, and marijuana) in the country to be $100.40 billion in 2006: http://www.whitehouse.gov/sites/default/files/page /files/wausid_report_final_1.pdf.

By comparison, a November 2013 report (http://www.arcviewmarketresearch .com) by ArcView Market Research, a San Francisco–based investor group that studies the legal marijuana industry in the United States, assessed the 2013 legal U.S. market alone to generate about $1.53 billion, with $10.2 billion forecast for the legal market by 2018.

Connect with the rapper Redman via his website: http://redmansworld.com.

A compelling essay about the possible appearance of cannabis in the Bible is found in chapter 2, "Early/Ancient History," by Chris Bennett, in *The Pot Book: A Complete Guide to Cannabis, Its Role in Medicine, Politics, Science, and Culture,* edited by Julie Holland, MD (Rochester, VT: Park Street Press, 2010). Some of Bennett's provocative essays appear online: "Kaneh Bosm: Cannabis in the Old Testament" (http://www .cannabisculture.com/articles/1090.html), "Cannabis and the Christ" (http://www .cannabisculture.com/articles/1301.html), and numerous others: http://www.forbid denfruitpublishing.com/Chris/Writings. I should add that rebuttals to Bennett's theo- ries are easily found as well.

15. THE NEW MARIJUANA ECONOMY

Admittedly, both of the stories—of the illegal grow and the Dopp kit at the airport— related to me were anecdotal, but according to the article "Legalization Complicate Po- lice Marijuana Investigations in Colorado" by John Ingold, *Denver Post,* July 14, 2014, (http://www.denverpost.com/news/ci_26147592/legalization-complicates-police -marijuana-investigations-colorado), local police are occasionally hesitant to seize and destroy marijuana from grows that they suspect are illegal, for fear of civil prosecution at a later time if they are wrong. It is unclear how prevalent this development is.

At the same time that editorials in newspapers such the *New York Times* (July 27, 2014) are calling for legalization on the federal level (http://www.nytimes.com /interactive/2014/07/27/opinion/sunday/high-time-marijuana-legalization.html), their counterparts at papers such as the *Washington Post* are opposing legalization (September 14, 2014) in the District of Columbia (http://www.washingtonpost

.com/opinions/dc-voters-should-reject-the-rush-to-legalize-marijuana/2014/09/14 /aca37112-3ab6-11e4-bdfb-de4104544a37_story.html).

In September 2014, the National Conference of State Legislatures noted that the 2014 U.S. Farm Bill included provisions that would allow certain institutions within nineteen states to grow hemp in pilot studies in university or state departments of agriculture settings. State policies may be found at: http://www.ncsl.org/research /agriculture-and-rural-development/state-industrial-hemp-statutes.aspx.

The list of nations that currently grow hemp was drawn from the following lists at the Hemp Industries Association (http://www.thehia.org/facts.html) and the European Industrial Hemp Association (http://www.eiha.org).

In the firing case I'm citing—"Wal-Mart Worker Fired over Medical Marijuana" by Eve Tahmincioglu, *MSNBC,* June 28, 2013 (http://www.nbcnews.com /id/35913492/ns/business-careers/t/wal-mart-worker-fired-over-medical-marijuana/# .VCc4vb7XE58)—the courts found that the twenty-nine-year-old man who was suffering from a brain tumor was not protected from firing because the marijuana law in his state, Michigan, does not regulate private employment.

The article "Medical Marijuana Research Hits Wall of U.S. Law" by Serge F. Kovaleski, *New York Times,* August 9, 2014 (http://www.nytimes.com/2014/08/10/us /politics/medical-marijuana-research-hits-the-wall-of-federal-law.html), nicely summarizes how science has been hampered by U.S. federal prohibition. My further understanding of this issue was enhanced by the articles in part 3, "The Clinical Use of Cannabis," in *The Pot Book: A Complete Guide to Cannabis, Its Role in Medicine, Politics, Science, and Culture,* edited by Julie Holland, MD (Rochester, VT: Park Street Press, 2010).

My comments on vape pens and e-cigarettes are drawn from personal experience and articles such as "Some E-Cigarettes Deliver a Puff of Carcinogens" by Matt Richtel, *New York Times,* May 3, 2014 (http://www.nytimes.com/2014/05/04/business /some-e-cigarettes-deliver-a-puff-of-carcinogens.html).

The issue of edible misuse by children and adults is not likely to go away in the future. The most famous case that drew media attention came in 2006, when a police corporal from Detroit and his wife baked brownies laced with marijuana the officer had confiscated from a suspect. His frantic calls to 911, in which he claimed to be "dying" or "overdosing" of the drug, went viral, leading to media ridicule and his 2007 resignation. See "Cop Who Made Pot Brownies Will Avoid Charges," Associated Press Report, May 11, 2007 (http://www.nbcnews.com/id/18587902/ns/us_news-weird _news/t/cop-who-made-pot-brownies-will-avoid-charges/#.VCdAY77XE58). More troubling is the possibility that children will mistake marijuana edibles for candy or baked sweets. The issue has been covered in numerous media stories, such as "Snacks Laced with Marijuana Raise Concerns" by Jack Healy, *New York Times,* January 31, 2014 (http://www.nytimes.com/2014/02/01/us/snacks-laced-with-marijuana-raise-co ncerns.html). The class action suit I discuss was covered prominently in the Colorado media. See the article, "Class-action suit grow against firm accused of handing out pot-laced candy at Denver County Fair," by Alan Gathright, ABC 7 News, September 16, 2014: http://www.thedenverchannel.com/news/local-news/class-action -suit-grows-against-firm-accused-of-handing-out-pot-laced-candy-at-denver-county -fair09162014.

16. THE CANNABIS RANCH

Readers can follow the progress of our project and see architectural drawings and plans at greenmancannabisranch.com.

INDEX

ABOUT THE AUTHOR

CHRISTIAN HAGESETH IS THE FOUNDER AND CHAIRMAN of GMC, LLC. Mr. Hageseth has worked in the marijuana industry full time since July 2009, when he founded TGM Beneficial Care, LLC, the predecessor company of GMC. Prior to GMC and TGM, Mr. Hageseth was president and chief executive officer of HIPP Companies, a diverse real estate investment and finance company, which he also founded. His other experience includes founding an ice cream company and working in several business development roles in the technology, advertising, and mortgage industries. Connect with him via Christian@americancannabispartners.com.